What people GHW

"Wildlife viewing is one of the fastest growing wildlife activities in the United States. Millions of people plan their vacations and recreation trips to include opportunities to see and photograph wildlife. One of the best things local communities can do to increase and promote tourism is to learn about the wildlife opportunities and promote them as part of the overall visitor package."
Raymond A. Rustem, Natural Heritage Unit Supervisor Wildlife Division, Michigan Dept. of Natural Resources

"The dunes have long been a strong draw for Michigan. Each year they bring millions of visitors to Michigan to experience their beauty and serenity, and we need to preserve this unique resource for present and future generations."
Leon Stille (R) Spring Lake, State Senator, 32nd District, former Mayor of City of Ferrysburg

"Of course I remember when I signed the Critical Dunes Protection Act into law at Kitchel/Lindquist Dunes Preserve on July 5, 1989. It was one of my pet projects while I was governor."
James Blanchard, former Democratic Governor of Michigan

"Ferrysburg is pleased to be able to be a part of this preservation."
Bill Herbst, Ferrysburg council member at the "trail birthday party" in 1990

"The biggest dilemma in writing *Michigan Wildlife Viewing Guide* was paring down the number of great viewing sites to a size that could fit into the book. By the final cut, Grand Haven had 3 sites included."
Phil Seng, author of *Michigan Wildlife Viewing Guide*

"Altho Kitchel-Lindquist Dunes Preserve contains no Lake Michigan shoreline, it preserves foredunes, classic interdunal ponds and wooded backdune. Situated in a heavily developed area, the preserve itself remains undeveloped."
Elizabeth Brockwell-Tillman, naturalist at Gillette Nature Center, P. J. Hoffmaster State Park and author of *Discovering Great Lakes Dunes*.

"A visit to Harbor Island is a joy to behold at any time of the year."
Roger W. Tharp, Harbor Island Task Force

"When I'm out shopping I like to come here to East Grand River Park to watch the wildlife in this peaceful setting."
Aneta Houts, Grand Haven, senior citizen

"For the first time in the 19 years I have been taking students to K-LDP, I didn't have to worry about the bus getting stuck."
Dr. John Shontz, Grand Valley State University Biology professor, after the K-LDP parking lot was built

"But like a navigator who charts a new course, we now know the direction in which we're going. We might veer off to the left or to the right ... but the direction for this island is now clear."
Ed Lystra, Mayor of City of Grand Haven at dedication of observation deck on Harbor Island

Also by Betty J. Mattson

Sky Enterprises **Herbarium Page Sets**

Coming in 2002

Making a Personal Herbarium in the New Millennium

Grand Haven Wildlife Viewing Guide

Betty J. Mattson,
author
Kelly Jewell,
illustrator

Sky Enterprises
Publications

Grand Haven Wildlife Viewing Guide

by Betty J. Mattson & Kelly Jewell

Published by *Sky Enterprises* **Publications**
805 Waverly Ave.
Grand Haven, MI 49417-2131
telephone 616-846-4254
FAX 616-847-0751
First printing: 2001

ISBN: 0-9707650-0-2

Manufactured in the United States of America.

We conserve what we love; we love what we know; we know what we are taught.
African proverb

Dedicated to:

Samantha Spring Cackler & Summer Lady II
who kept me "on the beaten path" thru
15 years of wildlife viewing
and
Robert Riepma
for use of his strong arm hiking the trails
and his strong brain in technical matters

Betty J. Mattson

Dedicated to:

my husband, *Arthur*
and my daughters,
Amber & Alexandria

Kelly Jewell

Introduction

Wildlife viewing has **become a great sport**, enabling people to relax, learn about nature, be outdoors, and often build "life lists" of birds, plants, or animals seen. The purpose of the wildlife viewing guide series, being developed for each state, is to enable people to learn where wildlife of different kinds can be reliably seen.

Grand Haven's 3 sites listed in *Michigan Wildlife Viewing Guide* offer a variety of birds, other animals, and plants that can be seen. Among the more difficult to find birds, they include Peregrine Falcon, Belted Kingfisher, Eurasian Wigeon, Black-crowned Night-Heron, Great White Egret, Great Blue Heron, 18 species of warblers, and many species of waterfowl.

Sometimes a good way to know if wildlife is present is to **study the habitat** a species requires or **observe "signs"** such as tracks, scats (feces), and feeding evidence that indicate the animal has been there recently. The patient watcher can then decide if it is worthwhile to wait for the animal to return.

Plant species of special interest are also available in Grand Haven's sites: North American Lotus and Pitcher's Thistle.

GHWVG is intended to be a **starting place for wildlife watchers**. You will definitely need field guides to confirm identification. *GHWVG* will give an idea of what species may be found and in some cases, the location within the site where they "hang out."

A "species out of place" may be seen, sometimes due to abnormal wind patterns. Just because a species isn't listed in *GHWVG* doesn't mean it won't ever be found here. And some of the species listed were only identified once or twice in the past 10 or 20 years of observations recorded that were used in preparing the species lists for this book, and hence are really unlikely to be seen.

Every effort had been made to make this book as accurate and comprehensive as possible. A revised edition is planned for approximately two years from original publication date. Your help is sought!

If you notice **errors**, either in scientific names or other information, please let us know as soon as possible. Lists -- of birds, plants, animals, and references -- were as complete as we could make them with the assistance of many area "experts."

Additional information as to species seen or any other pertinent facts, also personal experience stories, **would be welcomed.** If you have seen or experienced something in one of the listed sites, we would like to pass along your "adventures" to readers of future editions of *GHWVG*. **Please send** any additions, corrections, or information to:

Grand Haven Wildlife Viewing Guide
Sky Enterprises Publications
805 Waverly Ave.
Grand Haven, MI 49417-2131

Table of Contents

Order Bank for additional copies

Proposed Plat Map: Harbor Island, circa 1922

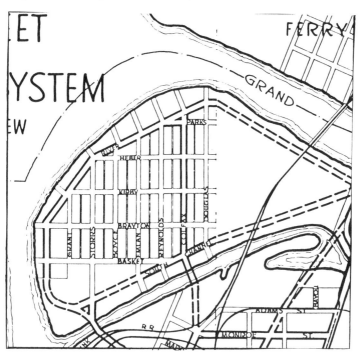

Kitchel-Lindquist Dunes Preserve Historical Background

The Kitchel-Lindquist Dunes Preserve is approximately 112 acres of duneland, located on Berwyck St. on Grand Haven's North Shore. Since 1988 it has been **managed** as a nature preserve by the **City of Ferrysburg**.

In 1971, 60 acres on the east side of North Shore Drive was donated to the Nature Conservancy by Mr. & Mrs. Gerald E. Lindquist and Harold W. Hartger. The property was transferred to the custodianship of Central Michigan University and named the CMU Dunes Preserve. After Connie Lindquist's death in 1980, it was renamed the **Connie Lindquist Dunesland** by CMU.

An adjacent 52 acre dune area was slated for residential development in the early 1970s, when local environmentalists, led by Marjorie Hendricks of Grand Haven, secured enough signatures on a petition to force a **referendum on re-zoning** the area.

In 1974, the Grand Haven electorate voted 2,167 to 1,075 to overturn the rezoning.

The area was already home to wildlife, including white tail deer. Twice, in the late 1970s and again in mid 1980s, the author was almost run over by deer while hiking on the site.

The Nature Conservancy, a national organization which lends money for the purchase of sensitive natural areas to preserve them, then negotiated purchase of the 52 acres. It contributed $160,000 of the purchase price, with $36,500 being added by the Lindquists. The area was named the **Kitchel Dune**, honoring John H. Kitchel, local physician and conservationist.

In 1980, with a **Comprehensive Employment and Training Act (CETA) Title VI project,** the Nature Conservancy developed and built a nature trail thru the area.

The project involved a dozen out-of-work county residents who **spread bark chips along the 3/4 mile trail**, placed wood retainers along part of it, built and installed benches and numbered posts to serve as interpretation points. The project was begun the end of Aug. and completed by Sept. 30.

The group also **built a boardwalk** thru a wet area where the water at times came up to the edge of the walk. Since the summer of 1988, the "wet" area has been mostly dry.

1980 was a hot summer that saw many severe thunderstorms in the area -- a year when huge trees were uprooted by high winds in Grand Haven's Central Park and other places. Both the City of Grand Haven and the Village of Spring Lake **donated their excess bark chips** for the building of the trail.

A **gravel shoulder** was built along the north side of Berwyck St. with gravel donated by Construction Aggregates.

While the trail and posts were completed in 1980, it wasn't until 1981 that the **Trail Guide** was completed. It was researched and written by the author for the Nature Conservancy and was made available free at Loutit Library in Grand Haven and Warner Baird Library in Spring Lake.

Bearberry:

In the spring of 1981, Dave Mahan, field representative of The Nature Conservancy, lead the **first public nature walk** on the new trail. He pointed out the scientific name of common Bearberry -- *Arctostaphylos uva-ursi* -- means "bear" in Latin. The group also saw a spring peeper.

Since that time many such walks have occurred. Some of them were for specific classes only, others were hosted by environmental and nature study organizations. Most, however, were open to the public. About this time Jeanie Griswold of Muskegon attended a hike where she saw her **"first ever Scarlet Tanager."**

Years later Griswold, by then an experienced "birder," still recalled that day. "It was way cool," she stated.

Scarlet Tanager

By 1988, CMU decided it no longer wished to own the Connie Lindquist Dunesland. The Nature Conservancy wanted to transfer ownership of the Kitchel Dunes to a local agency.

After Grand Haven City declined to take ownership, the City of Ferrysburg agreed to receive both tracts.

A **$300,000 Michigan Natural Resources Trust Fund Grant** was given to Ferrysburg to acquire the Kitchel Dune from the Nature Conservancy. CMU then also deeded the Connie Lindquist Dunesland to Ferrysburg. The **two tracts were combined** as the Kitchel-Lindquist Dunes Preserve.

With Deborah Apostol representing the state; Leon Stille, the City of Ferrysburg; and Executive Director Tom Woiwode representing the Nature Conservancy, funds and deeds changed hands.

The Ferrysburg City Council appointed a **Kitchel-Lindquist Dunes**

Preserve **Committee** to oversee the area. It was headed by Mayor Leon Stille. Over 30 people volunteered to serve.

Also in 1988, K-LDP was included in *A Natural Features Inventory of Ottawa County* and was "determined to have 3 notably significant natural community occurrences: Open Dunes, Interdunal Wetland, and Great Lakes Barrens."

The same year a "designated fund" with **Grand Haven Area Community Foundation (GHACF)** was established, enabling people to make tax-deductible contributions to be used in further enhancement projects at K-LDP.

By spring of 1989, the Committee had successfully acquired a **Coastal Zone Management Plan Grant** and hired Gove Associates, Inc. to research and prepare a Master Plan for the Preserve. Architect Richard Schaefer made several trips to Grand Haven for this purpose and the Master Plan was available for viewing in local libraries.

It included the original trail, later officially named the **Connie Lindquist Memorial Trail**, plus a trail along the nearly 1000 feet of Grand River water frontage, dubbed the "Arrowhead Plain Riverfront Trail," and a loop trail named "Interdunal Pond Trails." Also in the plan were a parking lot, restroom building, and observation platforms.

On July 5, 1989, Governor James J. Blanchard signed the **Sand Dune Protection Act** into law on the site, viewed by many area citizens and school children. In 2000, at a fund raising dinner for a Democratic U.S.

Representative candidate, the author had the opportunity to ask former Gov. Blanchard if he remembered when he had signed the Critical Dunes Protection Act into law at the Kitchel-Lindquist Dunes Preserve. His reply was, "Of course I remember that. It was one of my pet projects while in office."

The Committee held **trash clean-up bees, public trail walks**, and Earth Day exhibits. The group had slides of the area for showing to organizations wishing to learn more.

In 1990, the original trail was re-barked as a **Michigan Youth Corp.** project, supervised by the City of Ferrysburg. Bark was donated by the Grand Haven Board of Light and Power (BLP).

On Sept. 29, a **"birthday party"** for the trail was held at the site. Committee members, a representative of the Nature Conservancy, and community residents turned out for the event.

Later that fall, a **water main pipe** entering the land from the river in the dunes property, **broke**. Subsequent repair, conducted by the City of Grand Haven, caused quite a change in the immediate area, annihilating a sand bank "apartment house" for a colony of bank swallows and leaving a bulldozer wide lane of bare sand where vegetation had been.

In 1991 this was repaired, with plantings of Scotch pine and beach grass.

During the summer of 1991, a **sign** at the corner of Berwyck St. and North Shore Drive, marking the **entrance** to the Dunes property, was installed. **Private donations** provided funding for the sign.

Also during 1991, work was begun on the Riverfront Trail, with the help of a $8,550 **Youth Employment Services Grant (YES)**. With bark chips again obtained from the BLP, a 3,700 foot long trail was laid out. An observation deck was built as indicated in the Master Plan. Movable boardwalks offered three places where people hiking along the top of the river bank could access the beach area.

The **Kiwanis Club of Grand Haven** adopted the Connie Lindquist Trail as a project. By Sept. of 1991, trail signs were built by Advanced Signs of Ferrysburg and contained the information previously available only in the trail guide. On May 13, 1992, the 13 signs, replacing the numbered posts which had referenced the trail guide, were installed on the site by Robert Riepma and Bill Cansfield in the holes vacated by the previous posts.

K-LDP is home to **endangered Pitcher's Thistle, legally protected Bittersweet and Lady's Slipper,** sand cherry, puccoon, rock cress, Iris, false heather, Indian Pipe, and columbine. White tail deer, hognose and blue racer snakes, rabbits, many bird species, including waterfowl, turtles, and mussels have been observed or left evidence of their presence in the Preserve.

The area is used by local people for nature walks year 'round and also by school classes, from elementary level to college.

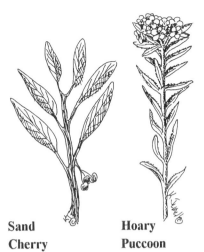

**Sand   Hoary
Cherry   Puccoon**

As an Eagle Scout project, Marty Neidlinger of Grand Haven researched, designed, built, and installed an **interpretive sign on the observation deck** along the Riverfront Trail. The sign commemorated use of the area by pre-historic Native Americans.

On April 14, 1993, the Committee sponsored a **public education program** to celebrate the preserving of this special sand dune ecosystem. The program consisted of a "mini re-creation" of the 1989 signing of the Sand Dune Protection Act by Gov. Blanchard. James Ribbens, Chief of DNR Land and Water Management Division, was the featured speaker. His topic was *Critical Dunes Act -- How it is Applied*. Also on the program was a video *The Michigan Sand Dunes* which was produced at Gillette Nature Center.

Former Ottawa County Treasurer Eunice Bareham, who was the Master of Ceremonies at the signing of the Dunes Act in 1989,

again served as MC. Representatives from local units of government, as well as environmental organizations, were on hand. These included Ottawa County Commissioners Peter Bol and Edward Bytwerk and State Representative Leon Stille.

Also during the spring of 1993, the K-LDP Committee cooperated with **Chautauqua** for an *Environmental Weekend*. Both a birding field trip, led by Judge Ed Post, and a wildflower field trip, led by Robert Riepma, were held here.

Cormorant seen on Ed Post walk:

When *Michigan Wildlife Viewing Guide*, a publication containing a network of wildlife viewing sites throughout Michigan, was considering sites for inclusion in the project during the summer of 1993, local units of government were advised they could "nominate" sites in their jurisdictions. Ferrysburg City Manager Dennis Craun arranged for the author to give Phil Seng, *MWVG* author, a tour of the K-L Dunes Preserve. Seng was immediately enthusiastic about the wildlife viewing available at the site.

By Feb. 1994, the Committee learned that Kitchel-Lindquist Dunes Preserve, along with Harbor Island, was chosen to be included in *MWVG*.

Over the years, school classes on all levels have visited the Dunes Preserve to learn about dune ecology. When **adult education** teacher Barbara Rowe of Grand Haven Community Education was designing a **course in "Environmental Studies,"** she wanted to include some "hands on" physical activity as well as book study. It was suggested that the class might "adopt" K-LDP for study, clean-up, and trail refurbishing. The following article was published in *Grand Haven Tribune* on Nov. 6, 1993.

"What began as a hands-on field trip for a community education environmental studies class is metamorphosing into a partnership with the Kitchel-Lindquist Dunes Preserve Committee.

"It started when dunes committee member Marjorie Hendricks visited the class in September. She talked about the site's history and showed the **Coastal Zone Program master map**, featuring bark-covered hiking trails."

Hendricks explained to the class the history previously recounted here.

"**After Hendricks spoke**, the class set out to continue the process. Their mission was to pull up invading spotted knapweed, a non-native plant, remove trash, and spread bark.

"Crew members were **appalled by the litter and debris** they found when at the site.

"Reacted Sheila VanVelzen: 'I learned how much we really do litter. Now when I go out with my family, I double check to make sure we take all our stuff, which I didn't always do before. I hope others will watch and take out what they bring.'

"Tina King and Susan Shaw were also shocked by what they found, things like toilet paper, bottles, cans, old clothing tools, a bathing suit in a bush, oil cans, automotive stuff and damage by four-wheelers.

"Tina Phillips couldn't believe how people treated the area. 'It was like a boaters' bathroom -- it was royally gross,' she said, referring to boaters who pulled their vessels up on the beach area.

"Old trash has been working its way to the surface for many years, a phenomenon noted by the Dunes Committee. The group has conducted clean-up bees since it began overseeing the site.

"Spring McPherson of Ferrysburg had one of the most interesting finds. 'Since I wasn't in class the day they went out, I went on my own to the site. Litter I found included a gas grill, lawn chair, and shorts dumped on the shore. I was walking along the river when I noticed something bobbing in the water.

"'I got soaked when I waded out to retrieve what turned out to be an old **peanut butter jar**. Imagine my surprise when I opened it and found a note and three postcards inside. It had been tossed in by a sixth grade **class in Holton** who were studying the effects of rainfall. The note asked to have one card mailed back to them and the bottle tossed back into the water with the other cards.

"'It is interesting to note the vast difference in ages of our two classes, but both are studying the environment.' McPherson said.

"Hendricks expressed concern about the knapweed at a committee meeting and when a member learned Barb Rowe was seeking a project for the environmental studies class she teaches, it was suggested maybe the two needs could work together.

"Besides demonstrating how to **idcntify thc knapwccd** and explaining how it crowds out more useful natural species, Hendricks led the students on side excursions to explore the area.

"'I knew the area was here,' McPherson said, 'but I thought it was only with special permission that people could hike here. Now that I know better, I'll come back often and bring others to see the area.'

"Hendricks said the students really got into the hardest labor of the project -- **re-barking the trail**. Ferrysburg crews furnished wheelbarrows and BLP crews stockpiled chips whenever they worked in the North Shore area.

"Moving some trees out of the trail area was another phase of the project which also included planting some native honeysuckle.

"Rowe, who has been teaching for Grand Haven Community Education since 1979, was asked to develop the class for this fall.

"'Our **goal is to understand environmental issues,'** she said. 'especially those affecting the Tri-Cities area, demonstrating the qualities of a concerned citizen, utilizing teamwork and effectively communicating our concerns and solutions.

"'Within this framework, the environmental studies class will focus on the impacts of water, land and air uses, energy sources, economic development, recycling, wildlife, aquatic life and endangered species.

"'We want instill an **on-going and life-long** empowerment of citizens who can better understand the demands upon the environment.

"'The class began its studies with sand dunes and surface water. Due to our visitation to the K-LDP, we were better able to understand that the area is the result of a long and complex **geographical and botanical history.'**

"The students enjoyed their 3 **excursions to the dunes**. 'I liked the hands-on experience,' said Jamie Batka who is working on his high school diploma. 'I'd rather be there than in a classroom with a book.'

"'I hope they will always keep it the way it is and keep it clean and not construct anything on it,' said Marc Santigo.

"Shana Watters was also impressed with the area. 'It feels good to help the environment and makes me mad that people who litter so much don't. We found beer bottles, cigarette butts and even plastic bowls. I'd like to see it keep its natural state

-- the way it's supposed to be is a beautiful setting.'

"The area will be more easily visited by classes like this after better parking is established.

"Rowe said 'We look forward to returning there in the spring for more clean-up, planting, or whatever else needs to be done.'

"George Romero expressed the class's feelings: 'It gives a good feeling. After we were done **we made a change**. It looked better. The class is more fun now, when we get to go outside.'"

In 1994 a **parking lot and entrance boardwalk**, respectful of dune ecology and adequate for several cars and 2 buses, was built on Berwyck St. Funding for this was provided by a Coastal Zone Management (CZM) Grant, $14,000; Committee-solicited donations, $8,000; GHACF, $6,000; in-kind donations, $500.

After the parking lot was completed, Dr. John Shontz took his GVSU ecology class there on a field trip and commented, "For the first time in the 19 years I have been bringing classes here, I didn't have to **worry about the bus getting stuck.**"

In 1997 **Harold Hartger's** land donation was officially acknowledged with his **name added to the sign** on the corner of North Shore Drive and Berwyck St.

Also that year new perimeter and parking lot signs were installed, as well as new signs on the Riverfront Trail.

New **trail marker signs** were constructed and installed as an Eagle Scout project by Brad Martin, noting only 12 significant points, instead of the original 15. This necessitated the development and printing of a **new "trail guide"**, which the Committee released in 1998.

The Committee sponsored a **"celebration"** commemorating the **10 years** of the K-LDP under Ferrysburg stewardship in Sept. of 1998. Trail walks were lead by Elizabeth Brockwell-Tillman and Dr. Bill Bond.

In Dec. of 1999 **Marjorie McInerney** donated 3 lots on North Shore Drive at the north end of the Dunes Preserve for inclusion in the Preserve.

With a $1,000 grant from the North Bank Communities Fund, a **"dunes ecology training"** session was held.

K-LDP Committee Chair Lynne Kinkema of Grand Haven explains some recent educational and care-taking activities at the Preserve:

"With assistance of Gillette Sand Dune Visitor Center naturalist Elizabeth Brockwell-Tillman and local naturalist Karin Neils, 25 docents were trained. Since that training the **docents have guided** hundreds of school children on field trips in the dunes. They have also visited classrooms in Muskegon and Ottawa Counties for pre- and post-dune hike ecology lessons.

"During the summer of 2000, the Ottawa County **Adopt-A-Stream** program, led by Dan Parker, brought 21 Johnson Control employees to the K-LDP to refurbish the trails. These employees worked for 8 days reconstructing the sand retaining walls on the trails, the viewing platform, and re-barking the trails.

"**Other volunteers** who have been active in trail maintenance are high school students from Grand Haven and Spring Lake, Shape Corp. Employees, and local volunteers during the 'Days of Caring Program' sponsored by the Volunteer Center of the Tri-Cities."

On Oct. 6, 2000, the former re-routed "Riverfront Trail" was **re-dedicated as the "Marjorie Hendricks Trail."** Marj explained, "I had to lay out that trail 3 separate times, as shoreline erosion washed parts of it away." A trail guide was issued.

The Committee in 2001 has needed to continue its **"protectionist" stance**, as the North Shore Marina has attempted to enlarge its facility and parking lot, with some proposed facilities coming as close as 20 feet to the K-LDP lot line. Ever vigilant, Committee members have attended the requisite public hearings.

Also the North Ottawa Water System indicated it needs to do additional work to **protect the water line as it enters the north shore** on K-LDP property. This would be necessary to prevent a reoccurrence of the water line break that happened in 1990. Repairing that break and re-installing the water line wreaked major havoc to the sensitive dune ecology.

The Committee continues to pursue development of the Master Plan. In the spring of 2001, Dr. Mary Kitchel pledged a sizable donation for the building of a **shelter/restroom building** adjacent to the Berwyck St. entrance. Architect Robert Landman donated his services to design the new restroom/shelter facility.

In April the Grand Haven City Planning Commission approved the site plan for the 1,408 square foot structure. Obtaining the remainder of the financing was being worked out as this book went to press. By the time it is published, work may be underway on the new building.

Kitchel/Lindquist Dunes Preserve
A good representative of Shoreline Dunes
by
Elizabeth Brockwell-Tillman,
author of *Discovering Great Lakes Dunes* and naturalist at P.J. Hoffmaster State Park

Altho this site contains no Lake Michigan shoreline, it **preserves foredunes**, several classic **interdunal ponds** and a wooded **backdune.** The site is situated in a heavily developed area of houses and summer residences, but the preserve itself remains undeveloped. The state threatened Pitcher's Thistle can be found here, along with a diverse host of other common **dune plants,** such as furry willow, sand cherry, red-osier dogwood, wormwood, common milkweed, bearberry, little bluestem, sand reed grass, marram grass, hoary puccoon, cottonwood and jack pine.

The flowering plants attract butterflies and other pollinating insects. This unique community is **home to a variety of animal species** including a diverse population of **Song Sparrow**

for breeding. The interdunal ponds also support the aerial hunting activities of dragonflies and many birds who rely on the rich array of insects for their nourishment.

Altho the natural processes that govern dune systems have been interrupted by **shoreline development** at K-L Dunes, the preserve is a unique natural area amidst a rapidly developing West Michigan.

Fowler's Toad

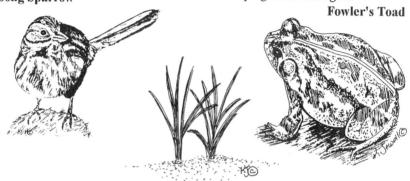

songbirds that nest among the shrubs of the open dunes and trees of the backdune.

During migration, the Kitchel-Lindquist Dunes, like all large tracts of undeveloped land along the shoreline, is utilized by **migrating** birds as stopover **habitat**. In the fall it is common to see large numbers of migrating hawks soaring above in search of a quick meal.

The classic interdunal pond habitat of the K-LDP supports plants and animals associated with **wetland communities**, but also includes a few rarities. Along the pond edges one can observe Brook Lobelia, Horned Bladderwort, Nodding Ladies' Tresses and several species of amphibians, including the **rare Fowler's Toad** who is dependent on seasonal waters

Butterfly Species of Kitchel-Lindquist Dunes Preserve

List supplied by Linda Koning

"This is a one day count on 8-1-00 with an addition of those specifically remembered and photographed. This butterfly species list is only a **sampling of the whole**. There are many more species than what I found -- some of which only live in early spring and many that might have come and gone already. Most butterflies only live a few days to 2 weeks; whereas, the Mourning Cloak and the Monarch may live up to 8 months or more."

FAMILY PAPILIONIDAE: tiger swallowtail, *Papilio glaucous*; spicebush swallowtail, *Papilio troilus*;

FAMILY PIERIDAE: cabbage white, *Pieris rapac*; clouded sulphur, *Colias philodice*; orange sulphur, *Colias eurytheme*;
FAMILY LYCAENIDAE: american copper, *Lycaena phlaeas americana*; coral hairstreak, *Satyrium titus*; summer azure, *Celastrina negelecta*;
FAMILY NYMPHALDAE: great spangled fritillary, *Speyernia cybele cybele;* pearl crescent, *Phyciodes tharos*; question mark, *Polygonia interrogationis*; mourning cloak, *Nymphalis antiopa*; buckeye, *Junonia coenia*; wood nymph, *Cercyonis pegala nephele*; northern pearly eye, *Enodia anthedon*;
FAMILY DANAIDAE: monarch, *Danaus plexippus*;
FAMILY HESPERIIDAE: dun skipper, *Euphyes vestris metacomet;* roadside skipper, *Amblyscirtes vialis.*

To have butterflies, it is necessary to have caterpillars; to have both it is necessary to have plants that are suitable as larval food sources and as nectar sources. K-LDP provides habitat for the above listed species.

Naturalist **Linda Koning** of Zeeland explains, "The preferred host of *Mourning Cloak* is willow. Hibernating over winter in trees and wood piles, it is often seen during winter thaws and again in early spring through summer. Frequently found on Coastal Dunes is the colorful *Buckeye,* which lays its eggs on toadflax. K-LDP has 2 species (*Linaria dalmatica* & *Linaria vulgaris*) of this host plant. Finding the *Roadside Skipper* was a special treat; it was an unreported species for Ottawa County. It nectars on asters, blueberry, and wild strawberry. The familiar *Tiger Swallowtail* has many host plants in K-LDP including willow, cottonwoods, and cherries. The common *Cabbage White,* introduced from Europe, is now one of the most abundant butterflies in the state along with the tiny little *American Copper* which is frequently seen along the dunes. Of all the hairstreaks in Michigan, *Coral Hairstreak* is the most commonly found. On the under surface is a beautiful coral band of spots reflecting the glory in which it was created. Some of the nectar sources for the Coral Hairstreak are blackberry, common milkweed, and strawberry. The host plants of the bright to light blue *Summer* Azure are dogwood, summer mints, and spirea, all found in K-LDP."

19

Butterflies of the Dunes:
with related caterpillars and host plants

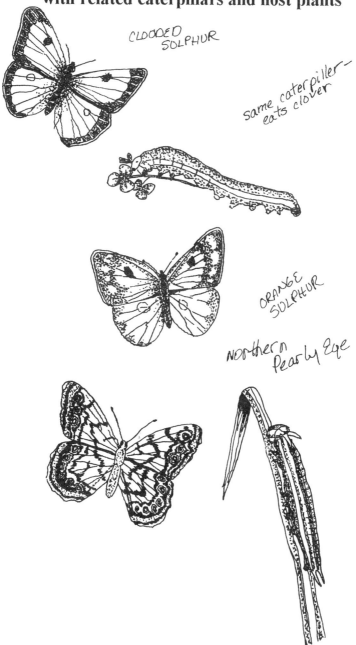

CLOODED SOLPHUR

same caterpiller— eats clover

ORANGE SOLPHUR

Northern Pearly Eye

Butterflies of the Dunes:
with related caterpillars and host plants

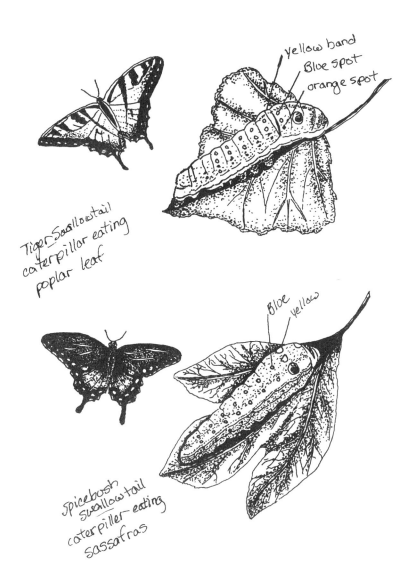

yellow band
Blue spot
orange spot

Tiger Swallowtail caterpillar eating poplar leaf

Blue yellow

Spicebush Swallowtail caterpillar eating sassafras

Harbor Island History:
From fishing to lumbering to dump to dredge disposal to nature preserve

The following account of early **"industrial activity"** at **Harbor Island** was published by the City of Grand Haven in 1988:

"Harbor Island was Grand Haven's first industrial park, and fishing was the city's first industry, dating back **prior to the coming of the white men**. Indians fished the waters of Lake Michigan for the purpose of obtaining food for themselves and families, and for trade with other tribes.

"**Large war canoes**, similar to the Sesquicentennial ceremonial canoe *Gabagouache*, were used in the fishing business. Somewhat crude nets were knitted by the tribe squaws. **Surplus fish**, which could not be eaten fresh, were split and **dried on racks** in the sun to be used later as food during winter months or to trade with inland tribes for other merchandise.

"When Grand Haven was barely 20 yeas old, in **1856**, two Milwaukee families moved here to establish the **commercial fishing business.** These Wisconsin Dutchmen built typical Netherlands' type fishing sailboats, about 30 feet long and with a wide 11 foot beam. Weather permitting, the large square sails were used, and on calm days, the fishermen were forced to use oars to reach their nets.

"As the Indians did, all of the **nets were knitted** by family members, with women and children busy the year around making and repairing nets. It wasn't until the 1880s that cork floats, molded lead weights and machine-manufactured nets eliminated much of the tedious work in the fishing industry.

"Sailing fishing boats were used until **1882**, when the Van Tol Brothers bought a **35-foot tug**, the *Merchant*, fitted with a crude steam boiler. Like subsequent fishing tugs, it burned slab wood for fuel, obtained from Harbor Island's many lumber mills. It wasn't until 10 years later that Captain John VerDuin purchased a fishing tug that used coal for fuel.

"About this time, hook fishing was introduced to Grand Haven and catches of sturgeon, from 50 to 200 pounds, were taken in large numbers. They sold for 2 to 3 cents per pound.

"In 1886 a whole **new branch of the fishing industry** opened when the firm of O'Beck and Baker set nets in deeper water, instead of in shallow water where perch were in abundance. They were astounded to catch hundreds of pounds of **"chubs"**, which were especially **adapted for smoking.** Firms owned by Dan Swartz, John Ruster, and H. J. Dornbos were the best known, and their smoked chubs found a ready market with daily shipments to Chicago."

Bruce Baker, descendant of the founder of D. Baker & Son Lumber Company, provides information on another significant historical "industrial" occurrence at Harbor Island in the 1870s: **lumbering.**

"In 1871 Derk Bakker and his brother, Jeltze Bakker, established the beginnings of D. Baker & Son Lumber Company, as a **lumber sawmill.** This business was situated near the present Third Street Bridge on Harbor Island in Grand Haven. Derk had come from the Netherlands to Holland, in 1844 when he was 4 years old. His family settled in Port Sheldon for many years before building the sawmill.

White pine was a frequently lumbered species, especially in the Muskegon area.

White Pine *(Pinus strobus)*

"The **trees** used by the sawmill were **cut down upstream**, near the Grand River, then the logs were **floated down the river** into the South Channel and processed into lumber at the mill, and shipped out by boat into Lake Michigan to its final destination. Derk's brother died in 1872, but the business continued in spite of the loss. In 1876 there were 17 sawmills on the Grand River in Spring Lake and Grand Haven, including 2 of the largest in the world. By **1890**, the surrounding **forests were depleted** and the town of Grand Haven experienced a drastic recession. Derk continued operating the sawmill until 1894, when a devastating fire forced him to begin operating as a retail lumberyard."

A check of the files in the Local History Room of the Loutit District Library turned up a **plat map dated 1922.** (see pg. 8) Apparently someone had intended to **establish streets** and possibly build houses or stores on the island. The project was probably abandoned due to instability of the soils and unsuitability for buildings.

The Island served as the **City Dump** for many years, finally closing about 1970.

A *Grand Haven Tribune* article in 1992 stated, "Residents regularly used the 23-acre dump area to get rid of junk, household garbage and yard waste." Area industries also trucked refuse to the landfill and the city used the area to dispose of dirt, chunks of concrete and other fill.

Ruth Drent of Grand Haven recalls trips to the dump with her father in his Model T truck: "I liked to go there. We went sporadically when he had something to get rid of or was looking to find something. I was probably about 8 to 10 years old at the time, probably in the early 1930s.

"There was everything in the dump: tires, batteries, big and small appliances, trash and household garbage.

"I remember there being lots of birds there, but I couldn't tell you now what they were. I also saw lots of muskrat houses, but don't remember ever seeing a muskrat itself."

Local sportsman **Larry Kieft** of Grand Haven recalls his boyhood experiences on Harbor Island.

"I hunted and fished on Harbor Island before fill was put in to make the road to access it. We could fish on both sides of the railroad tracks -- today that is all fill. There were lots of cattails, 6 to 8 feet tall; then it was a true marsh. I caught black bass and bluegills. Now that it is silted in there is more foliage and more feeding areas for waterfowl. But species diversity has lessened as well as total numbers. We used to see snapping turtles two to three feet in diameter. Some people caught them and made soup. Muskrats built their huts from the cattails found in the shallow water."

It was a **dredge disposal site** beginning in the early 1970s until the U.S. Army Corps of Engineers capped the former dredge disposal area in the

fall of 1996. The dredge Haines, which was used exclusively for disposal at HI, was towed to the Atlantic Ocean and sunk, where it now provides habitat for fish and other underwater animals.

The **Harbor Island Boat Launch** was created out of dredge spoils in 1948. This ramp is being expanded with grant monies in 1999 and 2001. Local boaters who didn't choose to use a commercial marina could launch boats there for day use. The Boat Launch parking lot was paved and striped in 1973.

In the early 1990s the City of Grand Haven established a **Harbor Island Task Force** to investigate "developing" the island and explore what the best uses might be. As a "recovering" natural area it was home to many types of wildlife, mainly birds.

In 1994 Phil Seng of Case Associates viewed the site with Assistant City Manger Mark Meyers and later recommended it for inclusion in the *Michigan Wildlife Viewing Guide*. His only hesitation, he explained, was that the "signage" showing how to get to HI was practically non-existent. "It would be helpful for local people as well as tourists," was his comment. He further explained that to list a site and have people attempt to visit it and not be able to easily find it would only be counter productive. Grand Haven Public Services Director Jerry Litzke, when presented with the situation by the author, suggested a Large Green Highway Designation Sign, which he later arranged to have installed. The promise of this, confirmed by Mark

Meyers to Phil Seng, enabled Seng to conscientiously recommend that Harbor Island be included in the *MWVG.*

Eurasian Wigeon *(Anas penelope)* a "disjunct" species seen at HI

Wood Ducks *(Aix sponsa)* **using nest boxes at HI have raised as many as 10 babies in one season**

Later a large elaborate bridge over the Island was proposed to be built, in spite of the fact that the additional traffic would diminish the quality of the wildlife habitat of this listed site. A **petition drive**, headed by Robert Riepma, garnered over 1400 signatures requesting that the **Third Street Bridge Gateway** be placed on the ballot. Instead the Grand Haven City Council sent out a "survey" to all registered voters. By a 3 to 1 margin, they nixed the Bridge.

Meanwhile in 1997, the city purchased the **oil storage tanks** and had them removed. In 1999, a replacement bridge was built to the island, a much smaller version of the Third Street Bridge.

Also in 1997, loosestrife eating beetles were released and began munching on the loosestrife. This aspect of the Island's history is discussed in detail in the section on alien species.

As the Harbor Island Task Force continued its quest for the best use, **observation decks were built** which make it easier for people to watch the wildlife, especially migrating waterfowl in the spring and fall.

Roger Tharp of Grand Haven, HI Task Force member, expert "birder", former high school biology teacher, and current employee of Grand Valley State University's Water Resources Div. who teaches on the research vessels that venture into Lake Michigan, shares some of his observations on the current natural history of Harbor Island:

"Over the last thirty years, I have seen Harbor Island develop from a city **dump** and **depository for dredge spoils** to a **recreational/ nature preserve**. I have had the privilege of being a decision-maker on the **Grand Haven City Harbor Island Task Force** for implementing the 1993 Master Plan for developing Harbor Island. We are fortunate that the City of Grand Haven has decided to preserve this great natural resource for future generations.

"The **convenient location** of Harbor Island is due to its close proximity to the Grand River, the Tri-Cities area, and U.S. 31. A person need not travel great distances with such **outstanding wildlife so close at hand**. While Harbor Island has been seriously degraded over the years, its great power of resilience has helped to make it a real 'jewel' today. Much community effort is helping this nature reserve continue to rebound.

Northern Shoveler

"Each visit I make to the Island results in new observations. In the past, I have been thrilled by the **spring migration** of Palm Warblers along the south shore of the Boom Pond. Many 'Kodak moments' have been created by seeing the male Red-winged Blackbirds brightly displaying their red-orange epaulets in order to attract females during spring courtship. It is not unusual to see more than ten Great Blue Herons patrolling the shore of the Pond during the summer. I have been honored by the presence of Blue and Green-winged Teal, Ruddy Duck, Northern Shoveler, Canvasback, and many Mergansers. In the winter, Mergansers have found the Harbor Island area a food bonanza. In March I have observed Rough-legged Hawks and Sandpipers passing through this area.

"Without a doubt, one of my greatest thrills was seeing a pair of Peregrine Falcons roosting for the first time on the City power plant smokestack in a provided nesting box during the year 2000.

"A visit to Harbor Island is a joy to behold at any time of the year."

Another person familiar with HI and its metamorphosis into a more stable natural area is Grand Haven resident **Aneta Houts**, whose late husband, Charlie, manned the toll booth at the Boat Launch for several years. She states:

"They have made wonderful improvements to **Harbor Island** lately. When my husband Charlie used to work at the boat launch ramp, I sometimes visited him there. The road out was very bumpy. But now it is nice and smooth and easy to drive on.

"It was not only bumpy but had clouds of dust from the dry gravel road. The small part that was paved was like riding on ocean waves. Many of the boat owners would complain about the dust and then the price to pay to launch their boats when they went thru the booth. Charlie would refer them to City Hall with their complaints.

"Now it is looking **so** nice. He would be proud, and I am too!"

On Sept. 18, 2000, all of Harbor Island was dedicated. Grand Haven City **Mayor Ed Lystra** made the following comments:

Peregrine Falcon

"On this beautiful day we mark a chapter in the history of Harbor Island. That history is partly a story of the Grand River, the longest river in the state of Michigan. It is partly a story of the Native Americans, who lived here in this place they called Gabagouache. It is partly a story of nature and the island's plants, trees and shrubs with the lesson that nature is not always our ally.

"It is the story of habitation -- the generations of people who lived here and what they **did with** this island ... and what they **did to** this island ... and more recently, what they **did for** this island.

"And it is the story of those who make their home here: God's creatures of the land and of the water and of the sky.

"For many decades there had been questions, debate and disagreement as to what this island should be.

"We have not answered all the questions. But like a navigator who charts a new course, we now know the direction in which we're going. .. A change of priorities, a change of direction takes a lot of work and I want to express **appreciation** for some of those of who made this possible: **Local teachers** -- kindergarten through university -- who worked and studied and advised on how to make this an educational setting; **City staff**; the **Army Corps of Engineers** -- without their cooperation this project would not have succeeded."

The mayor went on to recognize the contributions of other public and private organizations, individuals, and especially the Harbor Island Task Force.

"What is that 'sustainable philosophy'? Well, that's the subject of this chapter in the on-going story of Harbor Island. It is the **philosophy of stewardship** ... about us as a people -- living at this time, in this place -- taking responsibility for this island and healing the abuses which had been heaped upon it in the past.

"To all of you who were a part of this effort -- you can be proud of this accomplishment for a long time to come -- congratulations ... and for a job well done. Thank you."

In late June 2001, the Tri-Cities Historical Museum organized the first **"Feast of the Strawberry Moon"** held on HI. An 18th century "village" was recreated on the large field on the island. Almost 50 booths were set up, representing crafts such as rope making and log splitting, cooking, and minstrel and other entertainment programs. It is planned to be an annual event, **presenting** very **early history of the area.**

Harbor Island Task Force II is fine tuning the future of the island. During its long history it has taken many different turns; today it is a haven for wildlife, including endangered, rare, and migrating birds. People can view these species, sometimes from inside their cars, convenient during inclement weather and for handicapped people.

Muskrat "house"

EGRP: A lesson in history

Bald Eagles can be seen flying over the Grand River from EGRP.

Much of the "wildlife" that can be seen at EGRP is actually in the middle of the Grand River, flying overhead, or on the islands in the Grand River. They can be watched with binoculars or by taking a rowboat or canoe out into the river to see them closer. Today the **islands themselves** belong to Owashtanong (Owashtanong, often spelled different ways, means Far Flowing Water which was the Native American term for the Grand River) Islands Audubon Society (OIAS) and only their sanctuary committee members are allowed on the islands. Historically this was not so.

An item in the "75 Years Ago" column of *Grand Haven Tribune* dated Oct. 16, 1987, stated, "Wild rice was planted in the local marshes by area sportsmen to attract wild birds to the marshes for duck hunting season. The rice, a favorite marshland food of ducks, is expected to draw large numbers of them to the area." Counting back 75 years from 1987 would place the rice planting about 1912. Richard Klempel comments, "East End kids would notice wild rice growing in the marsh areas when we were young. It has all disappeared now."

John Klaver of Grand Haven remembers hunting on the islands. He states, "I've heard there used to be cattle on them; they were ferried across." He had observed ducks, pheasants, rabbits, and claims, "There used to be more ducks when I was trapping there in the 1940s."

The **Klempel brothers** grew up in Grand Haven's "East End" and remember a lot about the river. Clarence Otto is the oldest, then Wallace, then Richard. The 3 and Richard's wife, Lois, recalled the old days on the river for the author.

"Our father **trapped the islands in the early 1900s**, before WWI. One season the price of a muskrat pelt was $4.25. Fur buyers would meet trappers on the river banks, as they came in with the 'rats' they had trapped. They would buy their catch without their even being skinned.

Bale of "rat" pelts

"That year he trapped enough to buy and pay for the house we grew up in." They calculated he must have trapped over 600 muskrats, even at that high price. Some years as many as **3,000 muskrats were taken in a season** by all the trappers. When they wanted to display the skins, they fastened them to a rope, which covered the whole side of a barn. The photo of that is impressive. Otherwise the skins were baled and stored in the barn.

Later, the brothers report, the price dropped drastically, down as low as 80¢.

There was a **bounty on fox**. Richard shot one and received $5.00 for it. But fox were not often seen on the islands.

Red Fox

"There were **victory gardens** there during WWII." they said. Then there was growing hay. "The brush was burned off and nice hay grew up. When it was time to harvest, teams of horses and wagons were ferried across to bring the hay back. We used to grab some off the back of the wagon as it went down the street, to use in our rabbit hutches."

All 3 brothers and Lois claim the **river was so clear that fish could easily be seen** swimming there. "We speared them and strung long lines with maybe 150 hooks and caught a lot of fish, both in quantities and

number of species." The fish they report seeing and/or catching include: carp, bullhead, catfish, pickerel, northern pike, perch, sheephead, bass, sunfish, bluegills, dogfish and also mudpuppies, blood suckers, mudworms, and eels.

The river also had an **abundant supply of clams** which were harvested by clam fishermen who then sold the shells to a button factory near Lamont, where shirt and clothing buttons were made from the clam shells.

The **turtles** they saw included mud turtles, snapping turtles, leatherbacks. They used to shoot them with a .22 rifle and their mother would make turtle soup with the carcasses of the snapping turtles.

As to **birds**, they listed martins, teal, swallows, redwing blackbirds, mallards, wood ducks, mud hens, geese (during migration only), kingfishers, cranes, and shypoke, a long necked bird.

Except for the one shot for a bounty, they never saw fox, possum, raccoons, or deer like people do today. Once in a while a mink was trapped along with the muskrats.

Mink

They also had adventures with plants. Besides the wild rice mentioned in the beginning, Richard recalls, "The cattail plants are becoming much less numerous than they were when we were kids.

"Then we could cut the long stemmed cattails and have **cattail fights** when they were ready to blow off their seeds. You could throw them and they would fly like a spear, but it was more fun if you had about 3 in your hands and would club the other guys over the head or backs when they had run out of cattails and were trying to cut more. Then they would have to quit cutting and start covering their mouths and noses because the fuzz coming off the cattails made it impossible to breath properly. The 100% dark blue or black mackinaw coats we wore then had stable adhesive powers which would not let go of the fuzz. We would then have to sit and pick off the fuzz from our coats before we went home, so our parents wouldn't kick our butts for having cattail fights."

Larry Kieft's father and uncle once owned most of the big island in the Grand that now is managed by OIAS. Kieft hunted the islands as a boy and young man before they were sold to Michigan Audubon Society. He thinks they are **now much smaller**, probably due to wave action wearing away the edges. Once there were tens of thousands of Black Ducks to be seen, but now they are seldom seen. He states there was an "endless line of ducks along the shoreline, 500 to 600 at a time". He confirms that there are more geese today; in the past they were a rarity.

Canada Geese

"The **islands were dry then**; you could easily walk on them to hunt." He also recalls the victory gardens when his father owned the island. "People could have a plot with the understanding they would keep it free of weeds and not bother anyone else's plot. Violators were evicted." He also confirms the cattle grazing on the islands in the summer after the heavy vegetation had been burned off.

Trapping was a big activity. Between approximately 5 trappers, about 3,000 traps were set throughout the trapping season. There were **"trappers' huts"** built on the island in case bad weather caught one of the trappers and he had to stay overnight. Kieft calculates the trappers could only check a trap once every 3 days there were so many of them.

The shallow water promoted heavier cattail growth and hence, encouraged more muskrats. "'Rats," as they were commonly called, used the cattails to build their huts as well as eat and hide in.

Today with the wave action having **reduced the size of the islands** and with there being less area, cattails are also less dense. Muskrats have declined due to water pollution, habitat loss, and food source diminishing, to the point where seeing one is a treat, rather than catching 3,000 every year! Where potholes dotted the shoreline and provided habitat for waterfowl, those areas are now inhabited by marinas and provide "habitat" for boats and boaters.

When the **Michigan Audubon Society (MAS)** took ownership of the islands in the Grand River, the **Owashtanong Islands Audubon Society** (OIAS) was formed to oversee their stewardship.

In 1993, a crew boated to the perimeter of the property and planted **signs in the river offshore**, warning people not to tread there without permission.

OIAS member Fred Bevis states he believes most of the signs have now disappeared. He also states the group installed an Osprey Nesting Platform at considerable expense, only to have it "chopped down within 2 or 3 days of installation." He claims nesting on the islands has decreased since the loosestrife took over.

The City of Grand Haven acquired the EGRP property when land for the new Sewer Treatment Plant was purchased in 1971.

In 1975 approximately 6 acres was designated East Grand River Park. Facilities included there are: a public restroom building, picnic tables, playground equipment, a boardwalk thru a wetland area that allows close-up viewing of many wetland plants without getting wet feet. The park is served by a permeable surface parking lot, which reduces water run-off. It also contains a boat launch ramp, where citizens can launch small boats, kayaks, canoes, row boats, into the Grand River.

On March 13, 1995 the City Council voted to designate the boat launch ramp *Scott Flahive Launch Site*. Scott Flahive was a Grand Haven City Police Officer who was shot on Dec. 13, 1994, attempting to apprehend a prisoner who had just escaped from Ottawa County Jail. Naming the EGRP boat launch after him was considered an appropriate means to honor him, since as a boy he and his family spent time at the area and launched their kayak from the boat launch there. He was also an avid fisherman.

"When I'm out shopping I like to come here to **East Grand River Park** to eat my lunch, read, relax, and watch the wildlife in this peaceful setting. It is interesting to watch the trees change from season to season. There is also a small flower garden in memory of Scott Flavhive which I enjoy." commented **Aneta Houts**, a Grand Haven senior citizen.

The park affords an opportunity to observe the islands

and/or North American Lotus beds in the Grand River, which is easier if binoculars are used. It is also a convenient location to launch a small boat for a closer look at the islands or the lotus beds. While warblers inhabit the woods area during migration and the wetlands around the boardwalk often offer a close-up view of waterfowl, one of the main "wildlife viewing" advantages is the proximity to the Grand River and opportunity to observe, either with binoculars or from a small boat, the plants and animals that live and visit there.

North American Lotus Beds in the Grand River: An historical perspective

By Yvonne "Vonnie" Way

Yvonne Way of Spring Lake is the great-granddaughter of **Eugene Gardner**, who planted the original lotus in the Spring Lake area, located in Deremo Bayou, just off Indian Channel which flows into the Grand River. She has done much research into her great-grandfather's life and tried to determine where and how he obtained the original plants. She shares her research with us:

"By 1898 the forests were giving out and lumbering was all but depleted in the Grand River Area. As the family story goes, Eugene Gardner was sent by the lumbering firm to southern Michigan to **scout for** potential productive **forests**. While there he picked some lotus seed pods. When he arrived home, his scouting for new forests had been a failure, but he **threw the seed pods into Deremo Bayou** in front of his home. He was

hoping they would become a good source of food for the ducks.

"There was no sign of the elusive flowers for years and the project was given up for good. Then one day when Eugene was old and blind, his granddaughter, Esther Gardner (Robinson), brought in a newly discovered flower, took it to her grandfather for identification. He cupped the large, pale yellow flower into his two hands and stuck his nose deep into the bloom. As he smelled the beautiful scent, he exclaimed, 'Ain't it puddie!' The **seeds had lain dormant for about 18 years.**

"The lotus beds grew larger and larger each year and became a **tourist attraction**. The last weekend of July and first two weekends of August people drove out to visit the beds. The cars lined Boom Road all the way up to 144th St. These were very busy weekends and a good source of income for the Gardner family. The older hands took people for a **boat ride out into the beds**. Each person paid 10¢ for this ride. Others, not so daring, bought a flower on shore for 10¢ each.

"By 1936 I remember getting ready for the busy day early in the morning. We had picked the largest round leaf we could find and put it in a large wash tub with the edges drooping over the side. Also it was my six year old job to run around the farm to pick asparagus stalks to help beautify the wonderful blooms on display in their tall vases."

The lotus beds as an income source **lasted many years** for the Gardner family. Way continues, "Then, seemingly for no reason, the blooms became small and scarce, even wormy, soon to become non-existent."

She believes the Boom Road lotus bed **migrated down the river** with the current, to settle again and flourish along the south bank of the Grand River, near EGRP.

1991 was a good year for lotus, both in the Grand River and in the Mississippi River. Is there a connection? Possibly a "good year" in one part of their range is good all over. The author specifically remembers 1991 because she traveled the Mississippi River in Sept. and observed the healthy lotus beds there. The 1992 crop, like some of the earlier ones, according to Way, was wormy and small.

In 1993, when Michigan Botanical Club's White Pine Chapter sponsored an excursion with canoes into the Grand River from EGRP to see the blooms close-up, there **was a big healthy bed** of lotus blooms.

With binoculars people can really see them well. Using the Scott Flahive Boat Launch ramp, one can canoe or row out into the beds for close-up photography of this Michigan rare and legally protected plant. A dilemma for "wildflower watchers" is whether the year they choose to travel to EGRP to see the spectacular beds of pale yellow flowers will be a "good" year or a **"non-existent, wormy" year.**

Phil Seng, author of *Michigan Wildlife Viewing Guide*, commented on the lotus beds in East Grand River Park, "In Michigan they are protected, but in southern Indiana, they are so plentiful that they are actually considered by many to be a 'pest' plant."

North American Lotus (*Nembula lutea*) Bed in Grand River.

It is often possible to see everything from tight buds, partially and fully open blossoms, and seed pods all in the same "bed" at the same time, usually in early Aug. The 2 ft. in diameter, cupped leaves are held above the water and often trap insects. The blossoms are 8" in diameter. These are very different from "regular" water lilies.

GHWVG Birds -- all sites

K= **Kitchel-Lindquist Dunes Preserve**; I= **Harbor Island**; G= **East Grand River Park**; /// R= **Resident** -- lives here all year, may or may not nest here; S= **Summer visitant** -- is here during the summer, spends winters farther south in warmer climate; W= **Winter Visitant** -- lives here during winter, spends summers farther north; M= **Migrant** -- is seen here only during spring and/or fall migration, does not live or nest here; A= **Alien** -- exotic, introduced, or usually domestic species; E= **Endangered**; T= **Threatened**, per list adopted by Michigan Dept. of Natural Resources, March, 1999; * = seen only in low water periods

Note: This list is arranged in the taxonomic order of *The A.O.U. Checklist of North American Birds, Seventh Edition.*

Common Name	Scientific Name	Codes
GREBES/Podicipedidae		
Pied-billed Grebe	*Podilymbus podiceps*	**I-S-M**
Horned Grebe	*Podiceps auritus*	**I-M**
CORMORANTS/Phalacrocoracidae		
Double-crested Cormorant	*Phalacrocorax auritus*	**K-I-G-M**
HERONS, BITTERNS & EGRETS/Ardeidae		
American Bittern	*Botaurus lentiginosus*	**I-G-S-M**
Least Bittern	*Ixobrychus exilis*	**G-S-M-T**
Great Blue Heron	*Ardea herodias*	**K-I-G-S-M**
Great Egret	*Ardea alba*	**I-S-M**
Snowy Egret	*Egretta thula*	**K-I-M**
Green Heron	*Butorides virescens*	**K-I-G-S-M**
Black-crowned Night-Heron	*Nycticorax nycticorax*	**I-G-M**
WATERFOWL/Anatidae		
Canada Goose	*Branta canadensis*	**K-I-G-R-M**
Mute Swan	*Cygnus olor*	**G-R-A**
Wood Duck	*Aix sponsa*	**K-I-S-M**
Gadwall	*Anas strepera*	**I-M**
Eurasian Wigeon	*Anas penelope*	**I**
American Black Duck	*Anas rubripes*	**I-M**
Mallard	*Anas platyrhynchos*	**K-I-G-R**
Blue-winged Teal	*Anas discors*	**K-I-S-M**
Northern Shoveler	*Anas clypeata*	**I-G-M**
Northern Pintail	*Anas acuta*	**I-M**

Green-winged Teal	*Anas crecca*	**I-M**
Canvasback	*Aythya valisineria*	**I-M**
Redhead	*Aythya americana*	**I-M**
Greater Scaup	*Aythya marila*	**I-M**
Lesser Scaup	*Aythya affinis*	**I-M**
White-winged Scoter	*Melanitta fusca*	**I-W**
Bufflehead	*Bucephala albeola*	**I-M**
Common Goldeneye	*Bucephala clangula*	**I-W-M**
Hooded Merganser	*Lophodytes cucullatus*	**I-G-M**
Common Merganser	*Mergus merganser*	**I-G-W-M**
Ruddy Duck	*Oxyura jamaicensis*	**I-W-M**

EAGLES & HAWKS /Accipitridae

Osprey	*Pandion haliaetus*	**I-G-S-T**
Bald Eagle	*Haliaeetus leucocephalus*	**K-R-W-T**
Northern Harrier	*Circus cyaneus*	**K-R**
Cooper's Hawk	*Accipiter gentilis*	**K-S**
Red-tailed Hawk	*Buteo jamaicensis*	**K-I-R**
Rough-legged Hawk	*Buteo lagopus*	**I-M**

FALCONS/Falconidae

| American Kestrel | *Falco sparverius* | **K-I-R** |
| Peregrine Falcon | *Falco peregrinus* | **I-S-M-E** |

GALLINACEOUS BIRDS/Phasianidae

| Ring-necked Pheasant | *Phasianus colchicus* | **K-R-A** |
| Ruffed Grouse | *Bonasa umbellus* | **K-R** |

Meleagrididae

| Turkey | *Meleagris gallopavo silvestris* | **K-R** |

RAILS, GALLINULES & COOTS/Rallidae

*King Rail	*Rallus elegans*	**I-S-E**
*Virginia Rail	*Rallus limicola*	**I-S**
*Sora	*Porzana carolina*	**I-S**
*Common Moorhen	*Gallinula chloropus*	**I-S**
American Coot	*Fulica americana*	**I-G-S**

PLOVERS/Charadrlidae

| Killdeer | *Charadrius vociferus* | **K-I-G-S** |

SANDPIPERS & ALLIES/Scolopacidae

Greater Yellowlegs	*Tringa melanoleuca*	**I-G-M**
Lesser Yellowlegs	*Tringa flavipes*	**I-M**
Solitary Sandpiper	*Tringa solitaria*	**I-M**
Spotted Sandpiper	*Actitis macularia*	**K-I-G-S**
Sanderling	*Calidris alba*	**I-M**
Least Sandpiper	*Calidris minutilla*	**I-M**
White-rumped Sandpiper	*Calidris fuscicollis*	**I-M**

Stilt Sandpiper	*Calidris himantopus*	**I-M**
Short-billed Dowitcher	*Limnodromus griseus*	**I-M**
American Woodcock	*Scolopax minor*	**K-R**

GULLS & TERNS/Laridae

Franklin's Gull	*Larus pipixcan*	**I-M**
Little Gull	*Larus minutus*	**I-M**
Bonaparte's Gull	*Larus philadelphia*	**I-W-M**
Ring-billed Gull	*Larus delawarensis*	**K-I-G-R**
Mew Gull	*Larus canus*	**G-M**
Herring Gull	*Larus argentatus*	**K-I-G-R**
Iceland Gull	*Larus glaucoides*	**I-W**
Glaucous Gull	*Larus hyperboreus*	**I-W**
Caspian Tern	*Sterna caspia*	**I-G-M-T**
Common Tern	*Sterna hirundo*	**I-G-M-T**
Forster's Tern	*Sterna forsteri*	**I-M**
Black Tern	*Chlidonias niger*	**G-R-M**

PIGEONS & DOVES /Columbidae

Mourning Dove	*Zenaida macroura*	**K-I-G-S-M**
Rock Dove	*Columba livia*	**K-I-G-R**

OWLS/Strigidae

Great Horned Owl	*Bubo virginianus*	**K-W-M**
Snowy Owl	*Nyctea scandiaca*	**K-I-W**
Barred Owl	*Strix varia*	**K-R**

SWIFTS/Apodidae

Chimney Swift	*Chaetura pelagica*	**K-I-G-R**

HUMMING BIRDS/ Trochilidae

Ruby-throated Hummingbird	*Archilochus colubris*	**K-S**

KINGFISHERS/Alcedinidae

Belted Kingfisher	*Ceryle alcyon*	**K-I-G-S-M**

WOODPECKERS/Picidae

Red-headed Woodpecker	*Melanerpes erythrocephalus*	**K-R**
Red-bellied Woodpecker	*Melanerpes carolinus*	**K-R**
Downy Woodpecker	*Picoides pubescens*	**K-G-R**
Hairy Woodpecker	*Picoides villosus*	**K-G-R**
Northern Flicker (yellow-shafted)	*Colaptes auratus*	**K-I-G-R**
Pileated Woodpecker	*Dryocopus pileatus*	**K-R**

TYRANT FLYCATCHERS/Tyrannidae

Eastern Wood-Pewee	*Contopus virens*	**K-S**
Willow Flycatcher	*Empidonax traillii*	**K-S**
Great Crested Flycatcher	*Myiarchus crinitus*	**K-S**
Eastern Kingbird	*Tyrannus tyrannus*	**K-S**

VIREOS/Vireonidae

Warbling Vireo	*Vireo gilvus*	**I-M**
Red-eyed Vireo	*Vireo olivaceus*	**K-I-G-S-M**

CROWS & JAYS/Corvidae

Blue Jay	*Cyanocitta cristata*	**K-I-G-R**
American Crow	*Corvus brachyrhynchos*	**K-I-G-R**

SWALLOWS/Hirundindae

Purple Martin	*Progne subis*	**K-S**
Tree Swallow	*Tachycineta bicolor*	**I-G-S**
Northern Rough-winged Swallow	*Stelgidopteryx serripennis*	**K-S**
Bank Swallow	*Riparia riparia*	**K-I-S**
Barn Swallow	*Hirundo rustica*	**K-I-G-S**

CHICKADEES & TITMICE/Paridae

Black-capped Chickadee	*Poecile atricapilla*	**K-I-G-R**
Tufted Titmouse	*Baeolophus bicolor*	**K-I-G-R**

NUTHATCHES/ Sittidae

Red-breasted Nuthatch	*Sitta canadensis*	**K-S**

WRENS/Troglodytidae

House Wren	*Troglodytes aedon*	**K-I-G-S**

KINGLETS/Regulidae

Golden-crowned Kinglet	*Regulus satrapa*	**I-M**
Ruby-crowned Kinglet	*Regulus calendula*	**K-I-M**

THRUSHES/Turdidae

American Robin	*Turdus migratorius*	**K-I-G-S**
Eastern Bluebird	*Sialia sialis*	**K-S**

MOCKINGBIRDS & THRASHERS/Mimidae

Gray Catbird	*Dumetella carolinensis*	**K-I-G-S**
Brown Thrasher	*Toxostoma rufum*	**K-I-S**

STARLINGS/Sturnidae

European Starling	*Sturnus vulgaris*	**K-I-G-R-A**

WAXWINGS/Bombycillidae

Cedar Waxwing	*Bombycilla cedrorum*	**K-I-G-S**

WOOD-WARBLERS/Parulidae

Yellow Warbler	*Dendroica petechia*	**K-I-G-S**
Chestnut-sided Warbler	*Dendroica pensylvanica*	**K-I-S-M**
Magnolia Warbler	*Dendroica magnolia*	**K-I-S-M**
Cape May Warbler	*Dendroica tigrina*	**I-M**
Black-throated Blue Warbler	*Dendroica caerulescens*	**I-M**
Yellow-rumped Warbler	*Dendroica coronata*	**K-I-G-M**
Black-throated Green Warbler	*Dendroica virens*	**I-M**

Blackburnian Warbler	*Dendroica fusca*	**K-M**
Pine Warbler	*Dendroica pinus*	**K-S-M**
Palm Warbler	*Dendroica palmarum*	**K-I-M**
Bay-breasted Warbler	*Dendroica castanea*	**I-M**
Blackpoll Warbler	*Dendroica striata*	**I-M**
Black-and-white Warbler	*Mniotilta varia*	**K-I-M**
American Redstart	*Setophaga ruticilla*	**K-I-G-S-M**
Worm-eating Warbler	*Helmitheros vermivorus*	**K-S-M**
Common Yellowthroat	*Geothlypis trichas*	**K-I-G-S-M**
Wilson's Warbler	*Wilsonia pusilla*	**I-G-M**
Canada Warbler	*Wilsonia canadensis*	**K-I-G-M**

TANAGERS/Thraupidae
Scarlet Tanager	*Piranga olivacea*	**K-I-S**

EMBERIZIDS/Emberizidae
Eastern Towhee	*Pipilo erythrophthalmus*	**K-I-S**
American Tree Sparrow	*Spizella arborea*	**I-G-W**
Chipping Sparrow	*Spizella passerina*	**K-I-G-S**
Field Sparrow	*Spizella pusilla*	**K-G-S**
Fox Sparrow	*Passerella iliaca*	**I-M**
Song Sparrow	*Melospiza melodia*	**K-I-G-R**
Lincoln's Sparrow	*Melospiza lincolnii*	**I-M**
Swamp Sparrow	*Melospiza georgiana*	**I-G-S-M**
White-throated Sparrow	*Zonotrichia albicollis*	**K-I-G-M**
White-crowned Sparrow	*Zonotrichia leucophrys*	**I-M**
Dark-eyed Junco	*Junco hyemalis*	**I-G-W-M**

CARDINALS/Cardinalidae
Northern Cardinal	*Cardinalis cardinalis*	**K-I-G-R**
Rose-breasted Grosbeak	*Pheucticus ludovicianus*	**K-G-S**

BLACKBIRDS/Icteridae
Red-winged Blackbird	*Agelaius phoeniceus*	**K-I-G-S**
Common Grackle	*Quiscalus quiscula*	**K-I-G-S**
Brown-headed Cowbird	*Molothrus ater*	**K-I-G-S**
Orchard Oriole	*Icterus spurius*	**K-S**
Baltimore Oriole	*Icterus galbula*	**K-I-G-S**

FINCHES/Fringillidae
Purple Finch	*Carpodacus purpureus*	**K-G-R**
Common Redpoll	*Carduelis flammea*	**K-W**
Pine Siskin	*Carduelis pinus*	**K-W**
American Goldfinch	*Carduelis tristis*	**K-I-G-R**
House Finch	*Carpodacus mexicanus*	**K-I-G-R**

WEAVER FINCHES/Passeridae
House Sparrow	*Passer domesticus*	**K-R-A**

Approximate Spring Arrival dates for West Michigan Migrant Birds

Weather conditions have a decided **effect on migration.** If spring is warmer or cooler than normal, birds may arrive earlier or later than indicated in this list. Warblers usually arrive in "waves" with a warm front, and if warm fronts do not occur during May, observing warblers may be difficult. **Temperature averages** may also affect migration. Inland areas like Grand Rapids usually have higher average spring temperatures than areas like Holland, Grand Haven or Muskegon, which are nearer Lake Michigan and have cooler than average temperatures. This causes migrants to appear as much as a week earlier at inland locations than at lakeshore areas.

Many species of birds **winter in this area** more or less regularly depending on the severity of the weather. In severe winters, with several inches of snow on the ground, some of these birds will retreat farther south where they can find food. Species which usually **winter here** are those in the following list:

Mallard, Black Duck, Gadwall, Bufflehead, American Goldeneye, Common Merganser, Red-breasted Merganser, Canada Goose, Bald Eagle, Cooper's Hawk, Red-tailed Hawk, American Kestrel, Ruffed Grouse, Ring-necked Pheasant, Herring Gull, Ring-billed Gull, Great Horned Owl, Barred Owl, Screech Owl, Red-bellied Woodpecker, Hairy Woodpecker, Downy Woodpecker, Pileated Woodpecker, Horned Lark, Blue Jay, American Crow, Black-capped Chickadee, Tufted Titmouse, Red-breasted Nuthatch, White-breasted Nuthatch, Brown Creeper, Cedar Waxwing, European Starling, Northern Cardinal, American Goldfinch, American Tree Sparrow, Dark-eyed Junco, House Finch, House Sparrow, Snow Bunting.

Other species **arrive approximately** according to the following dates:

Feb. 20 to March 10:
Eastern Bluebird, American Robin, Common Grackle, Red-winged Blackbird.

March 10 to March 20:
Killdeer, Northern Harrier, Red-shouldered Hawk, Song Sparrow, Eastern Meadowlark, Rusty Blackbird.

March 20 to March 30:
Eastern Phoebe, Northern Flicker, Belted Kingfisher, Vesper Sparrow, Rufous-sided Towhee, Great Blue Heron, Common Snipe, Tree Swallow.

April 1 to April 10:
American Bittern, Greater Yellowlegs, Lesser Yellowlegs, Pectoral Sandpiper, Hermit Thrush, Brown-headed Cowbird, Field Sparrow, Fox Sparrow, Savannah Sparrow, Yellow-rumped Warbler.

April 10 to April 20:
Yellow-bellied Sapsucker, Purple Martin, Chipping Sparrow, Louisiana Waterthrush, Ruby-crowned Kinglet, Brown Thrasher.

April 20 to April 30:
Green-backed Heron, Solitary Sandpiper, Chimney Swift, House Wren, Barn Swallow,White-throated Sparrow.

April 30 to May 10:
Eastern Kingbird, Great Crested Flycatcher, Least Flycatcher, Rose-breasted Grosbeak, Bobolink, Northern Oriole, Bank Swallow, Rough-winged Swallow, Warbling Vireo, White-crowned Sparrow, Blue-gray Gnatcatcher, Gray Catbird, Wood Thrush, Veery, Swainson's Thrush, Black-throated Green Warbler, Palm Warbler, Black-throated Blue Warbler, Magnolia Warbler, Ovenbird, Common Yellowthroat.

May 10 to May 20:
Spotted Sandpiper, Ruby-throated Hummingbird, Scarlet Tanager, Red-eyed Vireo, Golden-winged Warbler, Canada Warbler, American Redstart, Northern Waterthrush, Gray-cheeked Thrush.

May 20 to May 30:
Black-billed Cuckoo, Yellow-billed Cuckoo, Common Nighthawk, Eastern Wood-Pewee, Acadian Flycatcher, Willow Flycatcher, Tennessee Warbler, Blackpoll Warbler, Cape May Warbler, Cerulean Warbler, Bay-breasted Warbler, Mourning Warbler, Indigo Bunting.

Above information written by **George Wickstrom** and printed in *Favorite Birding Areas* published by Grand Rapids Audubon Club. Reprinted with permission.

Migration explained

James Ponshair of Allendale, MI is considered by many to be the "premier birder" of West Michigan. He wrote the master bird list for Harbor Island. *GHWVG* bird list is coded with the **site** where each species has been seen, and **resident**, summer visitant, winter visitant, migrant, and **alien**, with * marking those few seen only during **low water periods**. The low water designations are from Ponshair's HI list.

Jim shares some of his observations about **migration habits**, "East winds are best along the Lake. **Updrafts** will produce hawks and other raptors over Kitchel-Lindquist Dunes. Of spring and fall migrations, **fall is the best time** to see waterfowl in this area because you will see more species. Remember birds travel 200 to 300 miles a day, then stop over for the night. A **south wind** is best during spring migration; the birds are coming from the south. Since southerly winds predominate in our area, we get good birding then. In the fall, a **cold front** drives the birds.

"With all the towers up for telephone service, thousands of birds are killed during migration at night. In the years to come with man's new inventions, wildlife is sure to suffer."

Migrating Waterfowl seen
at *GHWVG* sites

♀

Hooded Merganser

♂

American
Coot

Ruddy Dock

♀

♂

GHWVG Sites' Warblers

A bird **seen primarily during migration** in this area, there are 18 species that have been identified in *GHWVG* sites. Consult the **Master Bird List** (pgs. 37 & 38) to determine which species are summer visitants.

Exact identification can be a real challenge, even for experienced "birders". Since they migrate in mixed flocks, it might be possible to see several species at once. A good field guide is a valuable source of information on distinguishing characteristics. The best one for these birds probably is the Petersen field guide by Jon Dunn and Kimball Garrett: *A Field Guide to Warblers of North America*, which includes color photos, drawings, and range maps.

Since they **migrate at night and early morning**, it may take diligence to spot them. Various species listed in the migration dates information span the times from April 1 to May 30. Some years see earlier overall arrivals than others. The species illustrated here are the 18 found in *GHWVG* sites.

Warblers from the top: Left side: Palm Warbler, Bay-breasted Warbler, Black & White Warbler. **Right Side:** Worm-eating Warbler, Blackpoll Warbler, Pine Warbler.

TOP TREE: Clockwise from top center: Magnolia Warbler, Black-throated Blue Warbler, Cape May Warbler, Chestnut-sided Warbler, Blackburnian Warbler, Black-throated Green Warbler.

BOTTOM TREE: Left side: Yellow-rumped Warbler, Canada Warbler, Yellow Warbler. **Right side:** Yellow-throated Warbler, American Redstart, Wilson's Warbler.

"Special" Birds Seen at Harbor Island

Harbor Island is a wonderful habitat for many kinds of birds. At a dedication ceremony held in Sept. 2000 near the observation deck built by **Owashtanong Islands Audubon Society**, the speakers were interrupted several times by waterfowl ascending from the nearby pond into the air and then flying away, honking vigorously. "Isn't it nice to be interrupted by them?" queried Mayor Ed Lystra as he attempted to finish his speech.

Bird expert **Jim Ponshair**, of Allendale, has spent many hours observing bird activities at HI and other sites along the lakeshore, as well as inland. He draws on many years of such observations, and also extensive research, when he makes comments about unusual birds found at HI.

Black-crowned Night-Herons

"All herons have the habit of **'roaming' as juveniles**, after they have fledged and before they settle in their eventual territory. Black-crowned Night-Herons are no exception." states Ponshair.

This is the species featured with a photo in *Michigan Wildlife Viewing Guide* as representing HI.

Adult Black-crowned Night Heron

"During the summer of 2000," Ponshair continues, "I observed five immature Black-crowned Night Herons on Harbor Island, on several occasions. This is typical of the immature birds' behavior. Adults feed at Harbor Island regularly, year after year, and these young birds were checking the place out." **Immature Black-crowned Night Heron**

That they **seek out other areas to explore** was further observed by birder Robert Riepma, who lives across the street from a large pond within the city limits of Grand Haven, many blocks away from Harbor Island. Riepma positively identified an immature Black-crowned Night-Heron on that pond about the same time Ponshair was counting the ones on HI.

According to an exhibit at University of Michigan Natural History Museum, Black-crowned Night Herons retain their **"immature" plumage** until they are **3 years old,** which means those observed in Grand Haven might have been anywhere from 1 to 3 years of age.

These birds are most **active at night** and roost in trees and reeds during the day. They are most easily distinguished by their distinctive call, a loud *"Kwack"*. They fish more at night as their name implies. They roost in colonies like other herons and hence don't actually nest on HI, altho immature "roamers" frequent the site.

The adults are black above and white below, with the immature plumage being brown streaked over the whole body.

Peregrine Falcon

"It is believed Peregrine Falcons must be at least two years old before they **begin breeding,"** Ponshair explains. "They usually return to the same nest box each year.

"In the summer of 2000 a pair established a nest in a box on the **BLP smokestack** on HI. It appears that altho they built a nest, they didn't lay any eggs in it. It is thought the male and female were probably only one or two years old.

"The hope of birders is that they will return next year when they will be two and three years old. They may again build a nest in the same box and hopefully then they will lay eggs in it."

Ray Rustem, Natural Heritage Program Supervisor with Michigan DNR, advises, "Keep an eye on your peregrines on the power plant. They can provide a unique opportunity for the Grand Haven area if they return to nest."

How many years the same pair may return is questionable. Ponshair explains, "It is hard to tell how long a **peregrine's life span** is. Like most birds, there are so many hazards that for many birds getting to be 2 years old is called 'successful.' As birders know, the first year we lose over half the birds that fledge. The first year is always the hardest to survive, especially for birds of prey. The young must learn to hunt."

According to *Stokes Nature Guides on Bird Behavior, Vol. III*, peregrines usually lay 2 to 4 cream colored, brown-spotted eggs. Incubation is 28-33 days, with the "nestling phase" lasting from 4 1/2 to 6 weeks. The "fledgling phase" is at least 6 weeks and usually more. They only rear one brood per year. The female does most of the incubation, while the male does most of the food gathering.

Stokes states that **during mating**, peregrines "start a series of aerobic movements that may include steep dives, undulating flight, loop-the-loops, rolling over and figure 8's, all at incredible speeds. Occasionally the two may lock talons or bills in mid-air, after a chase. During courtship they also exhibit cooperative hunting, with one of the pair singling out a prey bird from its flock and the other diving for the prey."

Stokes warns that such behavior should be **observed only from a distance**, with spotting scope or binoculars, so as not to disturb the birds or interfere with their nesting.

While such behavior would be fascinating "wildlife watching", it is hoped that *GHWVG* readers will obey the caution to do so only from a distance.

Courtship takes place Jan., Feb. and March, with nest building from mid-Feb. to early March, and breeding from March thru July. Mate feeding -- the male bringing food to the female -- is another observable behavior.

In North America, the peregrine is migratory, flying south in Sept. and Oct. and north again in March and April, with **peak spring migration** from March 15 to May 10 in the central U.S.

From the 1940s to the 1960s, peregrines east of the Mississippi were eliminated. The bird overall was on the **"endangered list."** DDT and other pesticides were blamed. The prey birds they ate contained the pesticide contaminants which built up in the "top-of-the-food-chain" peregrines to the point where the egg shells were too fragile to withstand the parents brooding them. Birds have been released in our area in an attempt to reintroduce them where they once occurred naturally.

The pair at HI is considered special by area birders and hopefully will continue to return and nest there every year.

Chip Francke, naturalist with Ottawa County Parks, relates an experience observing the peregrines during the spring of 2001. This article is reprinted from *Far Flowing Water*, the newsletter of Owashtanong Islands Audubon Society, Vol. 11, No. 5, Feb. 2001:

"Peregrine falcons are an uncommon migrating raptor along the Great Lakes shoreline. On **January 21, 2001**, I was birding the Harbor Island area and was parked in the public boat launch parking lot. As I looked out over the ice, a peregrine falcon flew past my parked car and landed on the ice about 100 yards away. A few seconds later, I noticed another peregrine that was only 30 yards away from me. This bird was also on the ice and was standing on top of a freshly **killed male common goldeneye**. Using my car as a blind, I was able to look at this bird through my spotting scope as it fed on the dead duck. I noticed right away that the bird was banded and I was close enough that I could clearly read the numbers and letters on the band.

Common Goldeneye

"On its left leg was a two-color band that was black over red. I could see the number "8" in the black part of the band and the letter "U" in the red part. On its right leg, it had a pinkish-colored aluminum band with no clearly visible numbers or letters. After this bird had its fill of goldeneye, it flew off and landed a distance away on the ice and the other peregrine flew in to feed on the duck. This bird had a black over green band on the left leg with the number "5" in the black and the letter "L" in the green. It also had a pinkish aluminum band on the right leg. Both birds were in beautiful adult plumage.

"The following week, I contacted biologists at the **University of Minnesota's Raptor Center** and they looked up the data on these banded birds. The pinkish aluminum bands on the right legs signify that both birds were fledged in the wild, as opposed to being hand-raised and released. The black over red "8/U" bird was banded as a fledgling **male in 1998 at the Pleasant Prairie Power Plant in Kenosha, Wis**. The black over green "5/L" bird was banded as a fledgling **female in 1999 at the Pulliam Power Plant in Green Bay, Wis**. It was exciting to not only view these spectacular predators in action at close range, but to also learn their age and origin."

On June 6, 2001, DNR specialists were able to band the 2 female and 1 male chicks that hatched in the HI nestbox. The 32" by 20" nest box was placed 240 ft. up the stack 6 years ago. 2001 was the first time nesting occurred.

Ray Rustem speculates on the probable **diet of the HI peregrines**. "In city settings, they take a large number of pigeons which are readily available and easy to take. In Lansing, they have taken everything from pigeons to snipe and rails to yellow-billed cuckoos. They will key in on species during migration. Peregrines will take a variety of passerine birds, and in your area, I would expect some waterfowl take." Obviously, Rustem was correct about the "waterfowl take."

Low water level seasons bring special birds

Virginia Rail

Again, birding expert James Ponshair explains, "You might find some of the **marsh birds on the mud flats during low water** times, such as we had during the spring and summer of 2000. (These species are marked with an * in the master bird list.) During years with normal water levels, they wouldn't be seen at all." Both 2000 and 2001 have been extremely low water years. Altho this has posed problems for boaters at the HI launch ramp -- and has even caused the City to spend money to dredge the area -- it has brought these interesting birds.

Sora Rail

Ponshair continues, "They eat **snails, molluscs, earthworms**, and other various **crustaceans**, which they pick up in the mud when it is exposed."

The species of these birds that have been spotted at HI include: Common Moorhen, *Gallinula chloropus;* King Rail, *Rallus elegans,* an Endangered Species; Virginia Rail, *Rallus limicola;* Sora, *Porzana carolina.*

Kingfisher

A bird that is often sought for birders' "life lists" is the **Belted Kingfisher** (*Megaceryle alcyon*). They can frequently be seen at EGRP, but are most dependably **found on the power lines along the entrance road to Harbor Island** from southbound US-31. They often "patrol" a regular beat and this seems to be a favorite. In *Ramblings: Reflections on Nature*, Emma Pitcher describes their behavior: "A belted kingfisher poises, wings beating hard; then, when ready to dive, he closes his wings tight to his body and plunges into the water. He may also perch motionless in a conspicuous place, waiting for a meal to appear before he dives."

This 13" stocky body bird with the distinctive shaggy crest, is blue-grey above, white below, with a blue belly band; only the female adds a rust colored band also. Their call is a distinctive rattle. Their bills are long for catching and carrying fish and other prey.

Eurasian Wigeon

In the mid-1990s an **unusual bird** was spotted along the waterfront in Grand Haven. Eventually it was identified as a Eurasian Wigeon (*Ana penelope*). At 18 -- 20 inches, it is smaller than a mallard, an observation that is obvious since they are often seen together along Grand Haven waterfront, at Harbor Island, and even swimming off shore on the riverfront at K-LDP. It has a red-brown head, with grey body. It is considered an "uncommon visitor" to North America, usually found along the East Coast. It has **remained in Grand Haven** for several years, companionably associating with the mallards, wood ducks, and geese that inhabit the waterfront, often to the point of becoming a nuisance. It offers a chance for "birders" to observe it extensively up-close to add to "life lists." (picture pg. 25)

Great Blue Heron Research

One of the most interesting, visible and striking birds found in *GHWVG* areas is the Great Blue Heron, *Ardea herodias*. This bird, usually seen wading in deep water, is approximately 4 feet tall. In flight, its neck is curved, not held out straight like the Sandhill Crane. That is the field mark for telling the two apart while they are flying high.

Great Blues **eat primarily fish and frogs**, but also at times take small mammals, reptiles and birds. They **nest in colonies**, which consist of nests of sticks on platforms, usually trees, lined with finer materials. They do sometimes build their nests on the ground. They lay 3 to 5 pale greenish blue eggs.

Retired GVSU professor **Fred Bevis** of Allendale has been conducting **research on the heron population on the lower Grand River** for the past 10 years. In spring 2001, he stated, "Last year the population peaked at 106 birds.

"Three years ago in the heavy snow, the **rookery** on Linden and Leonard in Tallmadge Township was all but **destroyed**. Since then they have **established 2 additional colonies**, near Georgetown Township Park with 21 nests, and on Crockery Creek, near Maple Island and Leonard, with 55 nests. The previous one on Linden and Leonard has retained about 4 or 5 nests. Having more than one colony has apparently contributed to their **increase in numbers**.

"I watch and count birds at 40 stations along the Grand, spending about 5 minutes at each, so am pretty certain no bird is counted twice." In between his extensive travels, Bevis observes the "stations" about once a month. In the **10 years** of his research, **total numbers have grown** from 55 to 60 to over 100 last year.

What will 2001 bring? Bevis speculates, "The population may drop due to the extremely low water levels. I expect nesting to decrease this year. On Feb. 4, I counted 4, which had risen to 49 birds by the late March count, and 81 birds in mid-April."

Herons are relatively easy to see, if watchers look closely in the cattails and reeds; the birds tend to blend in with the vegetation as they fish at the water's edge. They are at Harbor Island almost every day fishing and often stay there even while being observed.

GHWVG Gull Species

Franklin's Gull

Little Gull

Bonaparte's Gull

Ring-billed Gull

Mew Gull

By Robert Riepma

Gulls can be large or small, white/gray or black-wing-tipped. If you see a large gull it is usually a **Herring Gull**, but look for a ring on the bill. If it has a ring, it is a **Ring-billed Gull**. If the gull is small, look for the color of the head and wings. It could be a **Bonaparte's Gull**. However, storms can bring in unusual birds from far away. An ocean bird could be transported to the Great Lakes.

Franklin's Gull, *Larus pipixcan,* is an **uncommon spring transient** in Ottawa County. This small gull usually breeds in northwestern North America, and winters on the Pacific coast of South America. The sightings in Ottawa county have been in April, May, and June, with fall sightings in Oct.

Franklin's Gull **feeds largely on insects**, both on the ground and in the air or on ponds. Their common call is a shrill *"kuk-kuk-kuk;"* they also make mewing and laughing cries.

The adult is a dark-headed gull, 14-15 inches long, with a 36 inch wingspan. The gray wings have a narrow white band separating the gray from the black wing-tips. The ends of the primary feathers are white. The tail feathers are gray, and the eye crescents are white.

It takes 3 years for a Franklin's Gull to mature. The first summer birds lack a white primary bar, and their bill and legs are black.

Franklin's Gull **nests** in freshwater marshes and lakes, usually **on platforms of dead reeds floating** in water 2-3 feet deep. Their eggs are 52mm long, buff or greenish buff, with sparse brown marks.

The **Little Gull,** *Larus minutus,* is the **smallest gull**, at 11 inches length, and 24 inches wingspan. It is an **uncommon transient,** and occasional summer resident in Ottawa County. This small gull usually breeds in Eurasia, and winters in the Mediterranean. It is a rare but regular visitor to the Great Lakes. It has bred in Ontario, Michigan, and Wisconsin. The sightings in Ottawa county have been from Sept. thru Jan.

NOT Gulls of the "Sea"

Herring Gull   Iceland Gull   Glaucous Gull

The Little Gull plucks food floating on the surface while in flight, and dives for minnows and insects. They are very tame. Their flight is tern-like, and their common call is a soft "*kek-kek-kek.*"

The winter adult is a dark-capped gull, 11 inches long, with a 24 inch wingspan, black bill and dark spot behind the eye. The rounded wings are pale gray above, dark gray to black below. The legs are red. In summer, the head is dark, the breast pink and the bill dark red.

It takes 3 years for a Little Gull to mature. The first-winter bird has blackish primaries, the second-year has some brown in primaries.

The Little Gull **nests in grassy lowlands** and freshwater marshes. Their eggs are 41mm long, yellowish/olive-brown/ greenish-gray marked with reddish- brown-gray.

Bonaparte's Gull, *Larus philadelphia,* is a common **autumn transient** in Ottawa County, occurring in **large flocks**. This gull is named for Charles Lucien Jules Laurent Bonaparte (1803-1857), author of *American Ornithology* and a nephew of Napoleon Bonaparte. He worked in the Philadelphia area as an ornithologist and biologist from 1822-1828. This small gull breeds in the far north of North America. It winters on both coasts as far south as Mexico.

Bonaparte's Gull **feeds** mostly **on insects in the air**, dipping for insects trapped in the water surface layer, and also eats fish. Their chattering call is a nasal *"cheer"*, or a low quacking sound. Flight is buoyant, with rapid wingbeats, and head held down.

The summer adult is a dark-headed gull, 13 inches long, with a 33 inch wingspan. In winter the head is white. The wing-tips are a flashy white, the bill is small and black, the legs red.

It takes only 2 years for a Bonaparte's Gull to mature. The first summer birds have a partial hood. First-year birds have a dark brown carpal bar on the leading edge of the wing, a dark band on secondaries, and a black tail band.

Bonaparte's Gull **nests in open coniferous woodlands near ponds** and lakes. Their eggs are 50mm long, buff marked with brown.

The **Ring-billed Gull,** *Larus delawarensis,* is a **common transient** and **summer resident** in Ottawa County. This small gull breeds in Michigan, and most of the northern US and Canada. It winters from the northern US south to Mexico.

The Ring-billed Gull is a **scavenger**, feeding on fish, worms, rodents, and bird eggs. They feed in parks, plowed fields, and at garbage dumps. Their common call is a loud, raucous mewing cry.

The adult is a white-headed gull, 16-19 inches long, with a 49 inch wingspan. Their yellow bill has a black ring, hence the name. The legs are yellow or pale greenish.

It takes 3 years for a Ring-billed Gull to mature. The juvenile birds resemble a Herring Gull.

The Ring-billed Gull **nests on the ground** among rocks or matted vegetation. They nest in **large colonies** in rocky islets or isolated coasts. Their eggs are 59mm long, buff white, marked with browns.

The **Mew Gull,** *Larus canus,* is west-coast bird, a **casual or accidental** bird in Ottawa County. This small gull usually breeds in northwestern North America, and winters along the Pacific coast from Alaska to California and inland. It also rarely winters on the Atlantic coast from New Brunswick to Massachusetts.

The Mew Gull **feeds on insects, earthworms, fish, molluscs,** crustaceans, and occasionally young birds, mice, grain, and garbage. Their common **call** is similar to the Herring gull, *"kuk-kuk-kuk"* or *"yucca-yucca-yucca,"* but higher pitched.

The adult is a white-headed gull, 14-16 inches long, with a 43 inch wingspan. They have a dark gray mantle, and the primaries are black-tipped. In winter, the head is washed with brown. They have a thin yellow bill and a dark eye.

It takes 3 years for a Mew Gull to mature. The first summer birds are washed with brown. The second year bird has a two-toned bill; the first primary has a large white spot.

The Mew Gull nests on rocky or sandy coasts and inland lakes and rivers. Their eggs are 57mm long, brown/olive/buff marked with brown.

The **Herring Gull,** *Larus argentatus,* is our **most common** gull in Ottawa County. This large gray-backed gull breeds across northern North America, and winters as far south as Panama.

The Herring Gull feeds as a **scavenger**, and is often found cleaning up the beaches. This is the common **"garbage dump gull"** and eats anything from garbage to berries. Their common call is a loud, clear, bugle-like *"hiyak-hiyak- hiyak,"* also a warning cry *"gah-gah-gah."*

The adult is a large white-headed gull, 25 inches long, with a 58 inch wingspan. The white head is streaked brown in winter. The gray wings have black-tipped primaries. Its bill is yellow, with a red spot. They have pink legs and feet, and yellow eyelids in summer.

It takes 4 years for a Herring Gull to mature. The first winter birds are brown overall, and have a dark bill and dark eye. The second winter bird has a gray back, and brown wings, and a two-toned bill, and white rump. The third winter gull still has some brown on the body and wing.

The Herring Gull **nests on the ground** or on cliffs, making its nest with seaweed or grass. Their eggs are 72mm long, olive/light-blue/cinnamon, or heavily spotted olive-brown.

The **Iceland Gull,** *Larus glaucoides,* is an **uncommon transient** in Ottawa County and a winter visitor. This large gull usually breeds in Greenland and on Baffin Island, and winters on the Atlantic coast of North America, south to New Jersey, and inland to the Great Lakes. The sightings in Ottawa County have been from Nov. to May.

The Iceland Gull **feeds where fish are cleaned**, also in garbage dumps, and on bird eggs, carrion, and berries.

The adult is pearl-gray to white-winged, 22 inches long, with a 54 inch wingspan. The pale gray wings have white tips that protrude past the tail. The ends of the primaries are white. The eye crescents are often yellow, but a few have a brown tint.

It takes 4 years for Iceland Gulls to mature. The first year they are a creamy-buff to mostly white, and their bill is dark, and their eye is dark.

The Iceland Gull **nests on cliffs** or sandy shores in Greenland and on Baffin Island. Their eggs are 68mm long, clay colored, with brown marks.

The **Glaucous Gull,** *Larus hyperboreus,* is **uncommon** south of Canada. This large gull usually breeds in the tundra, and winters in North America. The sightings in Ottawa county have been in Jan. and Feb.

The Glaucous Gull **feeds on fish,** marine invertebrates, carrion, small mammals, insects, and berries. They are **predatory**, known as voracious feeders, eating the eggs and young of other birds. Their common call is a hoarse croak or scream.

The adult is pearl-gray to white, 27 inches long, with a 60 inch wingspan. The wing-tips are translucent, and have no black in the tips. The bill is yellowish, the feet pink, and the adult eye has a difficult to see narrow red ring.

It takes 4 years for a Glaucous Gull to mature. The first winter birds may be buff or almost all white, with a bi-colored bill.

The Glaucous Gull **nests on rocky coasts** or margins, and islands in the tundra. Their eggs are 76mm long, buff olive, with sparse brown marks.

If you are still confused, do not feel bad. Some gulls seem to have the same problem! The Herring Gull will **hybridize** with the Glaucous Gull in Iceland, and the Glaucous-winged Gull in Alaska. The Glaucous Gull and Glaucous-winged Gull **hybridize** in the Bering Sea. The Iceland Gull will **hybridize** with the Thayer's Gull on Baffin Island. They must have heard the song, *"If you can't be with the one you love, love the one you're with!"*

GHWVG Swallow Species

GHWVG sites are home to 3 species of swallows.

The **Tree Swallow** (*Tachycineta bicolor*) is a small, 5--6-1/2" sparrow sized bird that has metallic blue or blue-green upper feathers and is white underneath. Its favorite food is bayberries. It may be observed playing with a feather, which it drops and then retrieves.

Normally it would nest in cavities in dead and decaying trees, but with the decrease in this habitat, it often chooses bluebird houses instead. For this reason, most bluebird trail instructions advise that the houses be set up in pairs, 100 yards apart. The swallows are territorial enough so that they won't allow another pair of swallows to nest in a house within about 15 feet, thus insuring that one of the pair of nest boxes will be available for bluebirds. The swallows

Tree Swallow on Bluebird Nest Box

line their nests with feathers where they lay 4-6 white eggs.

The **Barn Swallow** (*Hirundo rustica*) is the only one with a deeply forked tail. It builds mud nests, sometimes in barns and old buildings, hence its common name. But it very often attaches its mud structures to the undersides of bridges, like those found at Harbor Island. They lay 4-6 brown spotted white eggs.

The **Bank Swallow** (*Riparia riparia*) is the smallest at 4-3/4 to 5-1/2" in length. Brown above and dull white below, its breast is crossed by a distinct brown band and tail is notched.

This species breeds in colonies and usually tunnels into sides of sand banks along rivers, but may establish a colony in a gravel or sand bank left during construction. The side of a sand dune is a favorite place for their apartment houses. They tunnel 2 or 3 feet before enlarging the hole for the nest, which is lined with straw and feathers. They lay 4-5 white eggs. Like cavity nesters, these birds don't need camouflage coloring for their eggs, since they are hidden from view of predators.

Often the same birds return to the same sand bank year after year. At one time a long riverfront dune at K-LDP housed many pairs. It was destroyed in 1990 when the break in the water main entering the shore at that point was repaired, necessitating bulldozing the swallows' dune. In recent years they have established a new colony inland in a smaller sand bank at K-LDP.

GHWVG Swallow Species

Bank Swallow "apartment house"

Barn Swallow with "mud nest" under a bridge

GHWVG WOODPECKERS

Woodpecker "restaurants", dead, decaying, or dead "snag" trees, are one of the most common forms of "animal evidence" found in wild habitats. Woodpecker holes are erratic in pattern. If the holes are all in neat rows, they were made by the **Yellow-bellied Sapsucker**, which hasn't been found at *GHWVG* sites.

There are 8 woodpecker species that have been identified in *GHWVG* sites, beginning with the largest, the **Pileated** (*Dryocopus pileatus*) at 16 plus inches, solid black with a crested red head. It is more often heard drumming on trees than seen, with a *rat-tat-tat* sound that seems to carry for miles.

The **Red headed** (*Melanerpes erythrocephalus*) and **Red-bellied** (*Melanerpes carolinus)* are both about 9-1/4 inches long and inhabit open deciduous woods. See the illustration for the differences.

The **Hairy** *(Picoides villosus)* and the **Downy** (*Picoides pubescens*) are similar and it can be difficult to tell which one is being seen when only one is present. When both are together, it is easy to note the Downy is only about 6-3/4 inches long, while the Hairy is bigger at 9-1/4 inches. The Downy also has a shorter bill and can often be seen at bird feeders.

The final "woodpecker" is the **Northern Flicker** (*Colaptes auratus*), formerly called Yellow-Shafted Flicker. It too prefers open woods, but often is seen in town and eats ants on the ground as well as bugs inhabiting rotting trees.

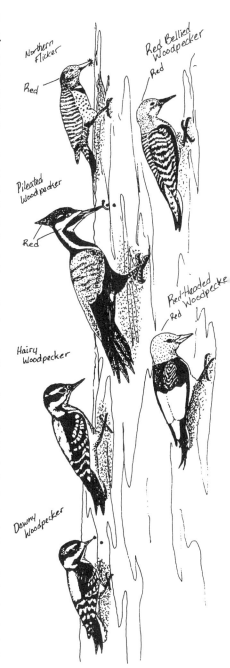

The Falcon & The Dove

The **Mourning Dove**, *Zenaida macroura*, is found at all *GHWVG* sites. Arnie Kelm of Norton Shores writes, "The dove mates for life. Mates feed each other. Incubating of eggs and feeding and care of young is shared by males and females. If one parent is incapacitated, the other will continue caring for the young until maturity. Both male and female will protect their nesting area.

Mourning Dove

"Mourning doves **reproduce slowly**. Only 2 young per clutch, which do not always survive. The Passenger Pigeon was a dove that became extinct despite great numbers here locally, and this from hunting. A dove has never been considered a menace to crops as other birds have.

"As a hunter myself, I see the mourning dove as a trusting and easy target." Legislation to legalize the hunting of mourning doves in Michigan is frequently introduced.

Former MAS president Tom Hendrickson explains why **hunting** mourning doves in **other states differs from Michigan**. "In our area they seem to be plentiful; we are on the northern edge of their range." While hunting in Indiana may not diminish the population unreasonably, hunting in Michigan would be another matter.

Another reason hunting mourning doves is dangerous to bird populations is their similarity in appearance to the **American Kestrel**, *Falco Sparverius*. As shown here, they don't look much alike, but in flight or sitting on power lines they are hard to tell apart. It is feared that the 10-1/2" Kestrels may be mistakenly shot for the 12" mourning doves.

The kestrel **divides its parental duties**: the male does all the hunting, while the female stays close by the nest, incubating and watching the eggs or eating prey the male has brought. It's unlikely that either would be able to raise the 4-5 young if the other were killed. Kestrels have been identified at both K-LDP and HI.

Peregrine Falcons' prey is exclusively birds, including the mourning dove.

American Kestrel

GHWVG Fish

Two species of fish have been positively identified (caught) at **Harbor Island:** **Carp,** *Cyprinus carpio* and **Catfish,** *Ictalurus punctatus.*

Originally native to Asia and Europe, **carp** were introduced to England where they became a popular "pond fish." It is from there that they were brought to the "New World" in approximately 1830. Further introductions were made by the U.S. government until they became well established in the wild.

Harrison Wallace of Muskegon Heights fishes frequently at HI and claims, **"Spring is the best time** to see Carp; they are spawning then."

Robert Riepma confirms this. "You can easily spot them roiling up in the *Peltandra virginica* when they spawn," he states. Wallace continues "Salmon eggs in the membrane and salmon sperm are the best things to fish with. Early spring, alewives are the best bait."

In late Sept., 2000 Wallace caught 10 catfish at HI. He exclaimed, "Catching 10 fish in one day is a VERY good haul indeed. **Fall is the best time to catch catfish** here. The largest I ever caught at Harbor Island was probably about 30 inches long. This is a good place to fish; I come here often."

Carp

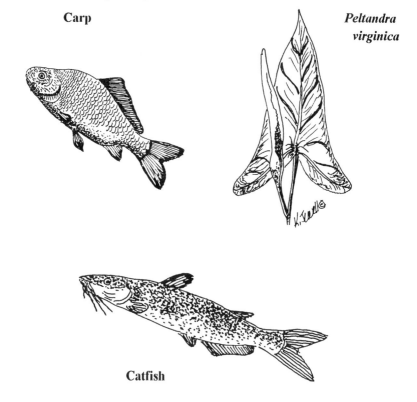

Peltandra virginica

Catfish

GHWVG Amphibians

GHWVG sites are home to 2 species of frogs and 2 species of toads.

Frogs include the **Bull Frog**, *Rana catesbeiana,* Michigan's largest frog. They have been observed at EGRP, an example of the permanent ponds, lakes, and marshes that make up their habitat.

Green Frog:

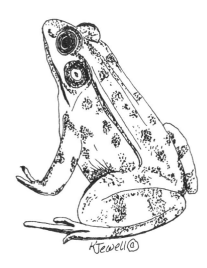

KJewell©

Adults range from 3-1/2" long to 8" long. They may be green, yellowish green, olive, brown, sometimes with scattered dark brown spots on the back; the belly is white, mottled with grey. Males have large eardrums and yellow throats; females small eardrums and white throats.

Males are territorial and may engage in "wrestling matches" over territory. Breeding occurs in June and early July, with tadpoles hatching 3 to 6 days after the **female lays** a mass of from **5,000 to 20,000 eggs.**

They usually overwinter as tadpoles and may not metamorphose until their 2nd or 3rd summer.

They eat insects, crayfish, smaller frogs, small snakes, turtles, mice and birds. If caught, they "yelp" or scream until released.

Green frogs, *Rana clamitans melanota,* are smaller (2-1/3" to 4-1/4") and have dorsal ridges on each side of their backs. Altho "common throughout the state," so far none have been positively identified and reported at *GHWVG* sites.

Bull Frog:

The other frog, found at K-LDP, is the **Northern Spring Peeper,** *Pseudacris crucifer crucifer.* At from 3/4" to 1-1/3 " in length for an adult, they are **one of the smallest** Michigan frogs. Living in trees, they are identifiable by the darker X shaped mark on the back. They are brown or tan.

Breeding is from late March until May. Females attach up to 1000 eggs to underwater leaves or stems.

These hatch in 3 to 15 days, with tadpoles becoming froglets within 2 to 3 months.

Their habitat is woodland ponds, marshes, and "floodings." The males "peep" loudly to attract mates and a chorus can be almost deafening. They eat small invertebrates, which they may find in trees and overwinter under forest debris such as leaf litter.

Spring Peeper:

grow to 4-1/3" with Fowler's topping out at 3-3/4". Brown, grey or olive, with dark spots on their backs, they are similar in appearance, but the American has only 1 or 2 warts in each spot on its back, while Fowler's may have 3 or more.

The American has a long trilled breeding call; Fowler's is more nasal sounding. Both lay their eggs in water where they hatch into tadpoles. Americans breed April to May; Fowler's prefer warmer weather, from Mid-May to Mid-June.

They eat insects, spiders, and small invertebrates such as earthworms. They may eat as many as 3,200 insects in a season.

Both can release **toxic skin secretions** if threatened or handled. They spend much time buried in sand or soil and hence may not be seen.

American Toad:

Fowler's Toad:

GHWVG **Toads** are the **Eastern American Toad** *(Bufo americanus americanus)* found at EGRP and the **Fowler's Toad** *(Bufo woodhousii fowleri)* at K-LDP.

Differences Outlined

While **similar in size**, starting at 2", the American Toad can

GHWVG Snakes

Four species of snakes have been observed and identified in *GHWVG* sites. One is the wildlife species chosen to be pictured in *MWVG* for Kitchel-Lindquist Dunes Preserve.

There is no such thing as a poisonous snake. If **you eat** something and die it is *poisonous*; if **it eats** -- or bites -- you and you die, it is *venomous*; even rattlesnakes can be eaten! And our sites don't contain any venomous snakes. But several of them do bite, and emit a foul smelling anal secretion as a defense mechanism. So it is probably good advice to admire and photograph, but not attempt to handle any snakes you find.

From coiling and striking, to playing dead, to smearing a person with foul smelling anal fluids, to being champion swimmers, the talents exhibited by *GHWVG* snakes are many indeed.

Blue Racer:

The **Blue Racer**, *Coluber constrictor foxi*, is the **signature animal of K-LDP** and one of the most amazing animals to see in action! Many animals with 4 or more legs can't move nearly as fast as this one, which has no legs at all! It is a real challenge for photographers.

Blue Racers grow to 4 to 6 feet in length and may be solid blue, greenish, or grey-black in color. Found in **open woods, meadows,** edges of lakes, marshes, and **dunes,** they **eat rodents, frogs, other snakes, birds, and insects.** Altho they don't "constrict" their prey in the strict sense, they do sometimes press larger animals against the ground while eating them.

Out of 17 snakes native to Michigan, 10 produce live young. The **Blue Racer** is in the minority which **lays eggs,** from 6 to 25, in rotted wood, humus, or moist sand, in June or July. They hatch in late summer.

This snake, if cornered, will **coil and strike,** biting, but remember it is not venomous.

Eastern Hognose:

Another fascinating snake with interesting defense strategies found at K-LDP is the **Eastern Hognose,** *Heterodon platyrhinos.* This is a stout bodied snake, growing only to 3 or 4 feet. It has dark spots or blotches on a yellowish background. It prefers sandy areas, but may hatch out in grass as well.

It uses its upturned nose to dig for its favorite food, toads. Also an egg layer, it lays from 4 to 50 eggs underground in early summer. They hatch in 60-70 days as 6" to 10" snakes. They instinctively use the defense mechanisms, even while hatching if necessary. The author once observed very small freshly hatched snakes -- they flopped over to "play dead," which is usually stage 2 or 3 of their repertoire.

The first line of defense is to **puff up its head** and it may even hiss and strike with its mouth closed, hence it is often erroneously called "puff adder." If this fearsome display doesn't scare off whoever is frightening it, it moves to plan B, **feigning convulsions** and smearing feces on anyone who has picked it up. The final act is to **"play dead"** where it flops over on its back. If righted again, it will merely flop over again.

EGRP is home to 2 different species: **Eastern Garter Snake**, *Thamophis sirtalis sirtalis*, and **Northern Water Snake**, *Nerodia sipedon sipedon*. Another thing these species have in common besides their home territory is **live birth.**

Eastern Garter Snake:

The **Eastern Garter** is one of 3 garter snakes found in the state and grows to 2 to 4 feet. It has 3 stripes lengthwise along its body. These are yellow, white, or green on a background of black, brown, or olive.

The belly is pale yellow, green, or blue.

The **preferred habitats** are woods, meadows, marshes, and lake edges, all of which can be found in EGRP. Its **primary foods are earthworms, frogs, toads, and fish.** The 6 to 50 **young are born alive** in midsummer. If handled, this snake may smear a restraining hand with an anal secretion.

Northern Water Snake:

The **Northern Water Snake** is found near **ponds, lakes, streams, and rivers.** It likes to sun itself on logs, **branches hanging over the water** and rock piles. If disturbed, it will glide into the water, where it is an **expert swimmer**, both on the surface and submerged. It also will emit a foul smelling anal secretion if it feels threatened. Its primary **foods are frogs and fish**. In late summer it gives birth to from 8 to 48 **live young.**

It grows to from 2 to 4 feet in length. It has dark blotches or bands on a lighter background, but older ones may appear black. The sides of the belly have red, orange, or black spots.

GHWVG Turtles

Four species of turtles have been observed in one or more of *GHWVG* sites. They are: **I-G**-Painted, *Chrysemys picta*; **G**-Spiny Softshell, *Apalone spinifera*; **G**-Common Map, *Graptemys geographica;* **G-I**-Snapping, *Chelydra serpentina*. Also turtle tracks of unknown species have been observed on the beach at K-LDP.

Painted turtles can often be observed **sunning on logs** in the Grand River or inlets near EGRP. Sometimes they come on land and can easily be caught. Remember it is illegal to remove any wildlife from a public park. Turtles kept as "pets" rarely survive because of their special dietary needs. Their short lives in captivity are likely to be very miserable.

Snapping Turtles lay eggs on HI, which they bury in the sand. These eggs are dug up and eaten by raccoons, opossums, skunks, and dogs. It is important to not allow dogs to roam unsupervised in natural areas.

When they hatch, the **baby turtles instinctively head to water** where, unless they are eaten by fish or other predators while they are still very small, they can grow to be huge and eventually reproduce. Their most **vulnerable stage** is when they are eggs. Snapper eggs may hatch anywhere from 50 days to 150 days after laying. Temperature has an effect on how long it takes; it also helps determine how many hatchlings will be male or female, according to James Harding, MSU turtle expert.

Turtles cross roads and parking lots in the spring to lay their eggs. It is good for drivers to be alert to a "lump" in the road, which may actually be a turtle. Avoid running over them if possible. It is an act of kindness to help the turtle across the road. Don't attempt to move an adult snapping turtle by hand. If you have a shovel in your trunk, a large turtle may be lifted on it and moved off a road.

GHWVG Turtles left to right: Snapping, Painted, and Map. Under the log in the water is a Spiny Softshell.

Eastern Chipmunk

Two interesting species of the squirrel family found in *GHWVG* sites are: **13 Lined Ground Squirrel**, *Citellus tridecomlineatus*, found at K-LDP, and **Eastern Chipmunk**, *Tamias striatus*, found at all 3 sites.

These two animals are similar in many ways and may be confused with each other and misidentified. **Similarities** include: small brown rodents with striped bodies; possessing cheek pouches for storing and carrying food; similar diets which include seeds, nuts, and insects; underground storage of seeds for eating later; living in underground burrows. Both are prey for foxes, coyotes, snakes, raptors, and feral cats and dogs.

Differences are the 13-lined also eats bird eggs and carrion, while the chipmunk extends its diet to include fruit. The **chipmunk** produces **two litters -- 2 to 8 --** of young each summer, the first being born about May 1, with a second litter born in late July or early Aug. The **13-lined** has only **1 litter**, of from 7 to 10. In both cases the young are naked and helpless when born and remain in the underground burrow for at least a month to 6 weeks before coming out. While the **chipmunk** is most **active in early morning and later afternoon**, the **13-lined** prefers the warmer times of day and comes out **late morning to early afternoon**, retiring early in the evening. This **time of activity and preferred habitat** are the best clues as to when and where they are likely to be seen. A really major difference is the

13 Lined Ground Squirrel

13-lined **hibernates** for about 6 months of the year, from Sept.-Oct. to Mar-Apr., just like the woodchuck does. Altho the chipmunk may go into a deep sleep with its body metabolism slowing way down for a period of time during the winter, this is really only a "torpor" condition, with the animal awakening occasionally, exiting the burrow and foraging or eating stored seeds and nuts. The **chipmunk lives a solitary life**, except for mating, and definitely prefers woods and brush lands. Even expert birder Ed Post confesses to being duped. He recites,

"I have looked into a tree to identify the 'bird' I heard chirping, only to discover it was a chipmunk." The 13-lined inhabits open grasslands and avoids woods.

The **"stripes"** also vary considerably. One reference states the **13-lined** ground squirrel really has 23 stripes total, 12 dark and 11 light. Its **stripes do NOT extend to the face.** The slightly smaller and chubbier **chipmunk has stripes on its face** and fewer on the body. Note the illustrations for differences.

Raccoons -- a dangerous animal?

Raccoons (*Procyon lotor*) -- found at all 3 *GHWV* sites -- are often infected with roundworms, *Baylisascaria procyonis*. This parasite is so **dangerous** that the International Guild of Taxidermy issued a warning to its members while working with raccoons. The same applies to anyone encountering one of these engaging animals in the wild. An Illinois study of over 700 raccoons revealed that 70 percent of the adults and 90 percent of the juveniles carried the parasite.

Dr. Kevin R. Kazacos, D.V.M, Phd., of Purdue University is responsible for much of the scientific explanation on the **life cycle and effects of the parasite**. The eggs are hatched in the raccoon's intestinal tract and are spread with defecation of the feces. Thousands can also become attached to its fur. Handling a raccoon is potentially enough contact for a person to become infected. The parasite, when it enters a human, migrates to the nervous system where it lays its eggs. Infections can occur in the eye. Larvae eat tracts across the retina, causing difficulty in seeing in the dark, restricted side vision, and loss of depth perception.

Dr. Kazacos claims sometimes symptoms don't show if only a few of the worms are present in the body. The severity and progression of the clinical disease depends on the number of *B. procyonis* larvae entering the brain, the location and extent of migration damage, and the size of the brain.

One larva in the brain of a mouse or small bird usually is fatal. In a human, one or a few larvae in non-critical areas of the brain would probably cause minor or no clinical problems. If enough are ingested, however, the **disease can develop rapidly**, causing sluggishness, muscle weakness, fever, tremors and loss of appetite, coma and death! All rodents, birds, and rabbits appear to be susceptible and are natural intermediate hosts for the parasite.

Since raccoons are found at all 3 *GHWV* sites, it is advisable to **avoid contact with them**, even the "cute" babies and especially any dead ones. Other animals can pick up the parasite; even our dogs may be carriers and should avoid contact with 'coons.

Dr. Mary Jane Dockeray, founder and former director of **Blandford Nature Center** in Grand Rapids, tells, "An adult that appeared to be sick was brought to the Nature Center. I put it in a cage and a few hours later discovered it had died. Before it did, it evacuated a fist sized mass of the round worms!"

Embryonated eggs will sometimes survive for years in soil and are resistant to all common disinfectants, so clean-up is essential. Large areas are best decontaminated by a portable propane torch. An article in **Zoonosis Update** for the *Journal of America Veterinary Medical Association* concludes: "The pet-owning public tends to be unaware of zoonotic diseases associated with pets and wildlife. The key to preventing human infections with *Baylisascaris* will be **education of the public** about this parasite and its potential health effects."

Consider yourself now to be "educated" -- handling raccoons, even dead ones, can lead to serious illness, blindness, coma and even death!

Other Mammals

Many commonly seen mammals may also be found in *GHWVG* sites. These include: **Eastern Grey Squirrel**, *Sciurus carolinensis*, which varies in color from light grey to black and ranges from 16" to 19" long, **K-G-I**; **Red Squirrel**, *Famiasciurus hudsonicus*, the smallest squirrel in its range, from 10" to 15" long, **K**; **Eastern Cottontail Rabbit**, *Sylvilagus floridanus*, **K-G-I**; **Opossum**, *Didelphis virginiana*, **K-I-G**; **Red Bat**, *Lasiurus borealis*, **K**; **Woodchuck**, groundhog, or marmot, *Marmota monax*, **K-I-G**; **Striped Skunk**, *Mephitis mephitis*, **K**; **Red Fox**, *Vulpes vulpes*, **K**; **White Tail Deer**, *Odocoileus virginianus*, **K**; and **Muskrat**, *Ondatra zibethicus*, **K-I-G**. There are undoubtedly species of **mice, voles, and shrews** at all the sites, but they haven't been identified or listed.

GHWVG Plants -- all sites

Symbols: K= Kitchel-Lindquist Dunes Preserve; **I**= Harbor Island;**G**= East Grand River Park; **A**= Alien species; **E**= Endangered; **T**= Threatened

Plant lists compiled by Marj Hendricks, 1984; Sylvia Birckhead, 1993; Linda Koning, 2000; interview with Fred Bevis, 1993. Some species may no longer inhabit the sites; new ones not listed may be present. Initials in **bold type** indicate site where identified and if alien (not native) species; common name(s) used for plant in regular type; scientific name in *italics*.

TREES

Common Name(s)	Scientific Name	Codes
Alder	*Alnus incana*	**G**
Ailanthus	*Ailanthus altissima*	**A-I**
Apple	*Malus sp.*	**I**
Ash, American mountain	*Sorbus americana*	**K**
Ash, white	*Fraxinus americana*	**I-K**
Aspen, largetooth	*Populus grandidentata*	**K**
Aspen, trembling	*Populus tremuloides*	**K**
Basswood, American	*Tilia americana*	**K**
Beech, American	*Fagus grandifolia*	**K**
Box-elder	*Acer negundo*	**G-I**
Butternut	*Juglans cinerea*	**K**
Catalpa (northern)	*Catalpa speciosa*	**A-I**
Cherry, black	*Prunus serotina*	**K**
Cherry, pin	*Prunus pensylvanica*	**I-K**
Cottonwood, eastern	*Populus deltoides*	**I-K**
Elm, American	*Ulmus americana*	**I**
Hemlock, eastern	*Tsuga canadensis*	**K**
Hickory, bitternut	*Carya cordiformis*	**K**
Hop hornbeam, eastern	*Ostrya virginiana*	**K**
Hoptree (wafer ash)	*Ptelea trifoliata*	**I**
Hornbeam, American	*Carpinus caroliniana*	**K**
Locust, black	*Robina pseudoacacia*	**A-I**
Maple, sugar	*Acer saccharum*	**I-K**
Maple, silver	*Acer saccharinum*	**G-I**
Mulberry, Red	*Morus rubra*	**A-I**
Northern white cedar	*Thuja occidentalis*	**I**
Oak, northern red	*Quercus rubra*	**K**
Oak, white	*Quercus alba*	**K**
Pine, jack	*Pinus banksiana*	**K**
Pine, pitch	*Pinus rigida*	**K**
Pine, red	*Pinus resinosa*	**K**
Pine, Scotch	*Pinus sylvestris*	**K**

Common Name	Scientific Name	Codes
Pine, eastern white	*Pinus strobus*	K
White (silver) poplar	*Populus alba*	A-I
Poplar	*Populus deltoides*	G
Sassafras	*Sassafras albidum*	K
Walnut, black	*Juglans nigra*	I-K
Willow, black	*Salix nigra*	I
Willow, weeping	*Salix babylonica*	G-I

SHRUBS & VINES

Common Name	Scientific Name	Codes
Barberry, common	*Berberis vulgaris*	K
Bittersweet, American	*Celastrus scandens*	K
Blackberry, common	*Rubus allegheniensis*	K-I
Blueberry	*Vaccinium spp.*	K
Burdock, common	*Arctium minus*	K-I
Button ball, bush	*Cephalanthus occidentalis*	K-G
Buttonbush	*Lonicera sp.*	I
Cedar, northern white	*Thuja occidentalis*	K
Cherry, choke	*Prunus virginiana*	K
Cherry, sand	*Prunus pumila*	K
Currant, American black	*Ribes americanum*	I-K
Currant, swamp red	*Ribes triste*	G
Cranberry, highbush	*Viburnum trilobum*	I-G
Dogwood, alternate leaved	*Cornus alternifolia*	K
Dogwood, flowering	*Cornus florida*	K
Dogwood, red osier	*Cornus stolonifera*	I-K
Elderberry	*Sambucus canadensis*	I-G
Grape, wild	*Vitis spp.*	I-G-K
Grape, riverbank	*Vitis riparia Michaux*	K
Greenbriar, common, Catbriar	*Smilax rotundifolia*	K
Honeysuckle, American fly	*Lonicera canadensis*	K
Honeysuckle, smooth-leaved	*Lonicera dioica*	K
Honeysuckle	*Lonicera tatarica*	A-G
Hoptree, common	*Ptelea trifoliata*	K
Juniper, common	*Juniperus communis*	K
Michigan Holly,Winterberry, Black alder	*Ilex verticillata*	K
Poison ivy	*Rhus radicans*	K-I
Privet	*Ligustrum vulgare*	G-A
Raspberry, wild red	*Rubus idaeus striqosus*	K-I
Rose	*Rosa, sp.*	G
Rose, multiflora	*Rosa multiflora*	K
Rose, Rugosa	*Rosa rugosa*	A-I
Running strawberry bush	*Euonymus obovata*	K
Spicebush	*Lindera benzoin*	K

Steeplebush	*Spiraea tomentosa*	**K**
Sumac, staghorn	*Rhus typhina*	**K-I-G**
Virburnum, maple leaf	*Viburnum acerifolium*	**K**
Willow	*Salix spp.*	**K-I-G**
Willow, sandbar	*Salix interior*	**I**
Winterberry, Michigan Holly, Black alder	*Ilex verticillata*	**K**
Witch hazel	*Hamamelis virginiana*	**G-K**
Woodbine, Virginia creeper	*Parthenocissus quinquefolia*	**K-I**
Yew, American	*Taxus canadensis*	**K**

FORBS, GRASSES & MISC.

Common Name	Scientific Name	Codes
Alyssum, hoary	*Berteroa incana*	**I-A**
Arrowhead	*Sagittaria sp.*	**I**
Arrow arum	*Peltandra virginica*	**G**
Aster, New England	*Aster novae-angliae*	**K**
Aster, white	*Aster sp.*	**I**
Baneberry, white	*Actaea pachypoda*	**K**
Beach grass, American, Marram grass	*Ammophila breirligulata*	**K**
Beach grass, little bluestem	*Andropogon scoparius*	**K**
Bearberry, common	*Arctostaphylos uva-ursi*	**K**
Beechdrops	*Epifagus virginiana*	**K**
Bellwort, large flowered	*Uvularia grandiflora*	**K**
Bergamot, wild	*Monarda fistulosa*	**K**
Black eyed Susan	*Rudbeckia hirta*	**I**
Bladderwort, horned	*Utricularia cornuta*	**K**
Bloodroot	*Sanguinaria canadensis*	**K**
Bluets	*Houstonia caerulea*	**K**
Blue-eyed grass, pointed	*Sisyrinchium augustifolium*	**K**
Blue flag	*Iris versicolor*	**K-I**
Blue flag, slender	*Iris prismatica*	**I**
Blue vervain	*Verbena hastata*	**K-I**
Bindweed	*Callystegia sepium*	**G**
Broomrape, clustered	*Orobanche fasciculata*	**K**
Boneset	*Eupatorium perfoliatum*	**K-I-G**
Bouncing bet, Soapwort	*Saponaria officinalis*	**I-G-K-A**
Bugleweed	*Lycopus virginicus*	**K**
Bugseed	*Corispermum hyssopifolium L.*	**K**
Bulrush, softstem	*Scirpus validus*	**I**
Bulrush, slender	*Scirpus heterochaetus*	**I**
Burreed	*Sparganium sp.*	**I**
Bur-marigolds	*Bidens sp.*	**I**
Butter-and-eggs, wild snapdragon	*Linaria vulgaris*	**K-I-A**
Campion, bladder	*Silene cucubalus*	**K-A**

Campion, white	*Lychnis alba*	**K-I-A**
Catnip	*Nepeta cataria*	**A-I**
Cat's ear	*Hypochoeris radicata*	**K**
Cattail	*Typha latifolia*	**K-I-G**
Narrowleaf cattail	*Typha angustifolia*	**I-G**
Hybrid of 2 previous	*Typha glauca*	**I-G**
Centaury	*Centaurium erythraea Rafn.*	**K**
Chicory	*Chichorium intybus*	**A-I-K**
Cinquefoil, common	*Potentilla simplex*	**K-I**
Cinquefoil, marsh	*Potentilla palustris*	**K**
Cleavers	*Galium aparine*	**K**
Clover	*Lespedeza sp.*	**G**
Clover, Rabbit's-foot	*Trifolium arvense*	**A-I**
Clover, Red	*Trifolium pratense*	**A-I-K**
Clover, white sweet	*Melilotus alba*	**A-I-K**
Clover, yellow sweet	*Melilotus officinalis*	**A-I-K**
Clubmoss, shining	*Lycopodium lucidulum*	**K**
Cocklebur	*Xanthium strumarium*	**K**
Columbine	*Aquileqia canadensis*	**K**
Coralroot, Autumn	*Corallorrhiza odontorhiza*	**K**
Coralroot, spotted; large Corair	*Corallorhiza maculata (Raf.)*	**K**
Cow parsnip	*Aralia gigantica*	**G-A**
Cow-wheat	*Melampyrum lineare*	**K**
Cress, rock; Sand cress	*Arabis lyrata*	**K**
Daisy, ox-eye	*Chrysanthemum leucanthemum*	**A-I-K**
Dandelion, common	*Taraxacum officinale*	**K-I-G-A**
Dogbane, spreading (Indian Hemp)	*Apocynum androsaemifolium*	**I-K**
Dock	*Rumex sp.*	**I-G**
Dodder	*Cuscuta gronovii*	**G**
Duckweed	*Spirodella polyrhiza*	**G**
Duckweed	*Lemna sp.*	**I**
Dutchman's breeches	*Dicentra cucullaria*	**K**
Everlasting, clammy	*Gnaphalium macounii*	**K**
Everlasting, sweet	*Gnaphalium obtusifolium*	**K**
Fern, bracken	*Pteridium aquilinum*	**K**
Fern, Christmas	*Polystichium acrostichoides*	**K**
Fern, oak	*Gymnocarpium dryopteris*	**K**
Field pepper grass	*Lepidium campestre*	**A-I**
Fleabane, common	*Erigeron philadelphicus*	**K**
Fleabane, daisy	*Erigeron annuus*	**K**
Four-o-clock	*Myrabilis nyctaginea*	**I**
Foxglove, smooth false	*Gerardia laevigata*	**K**
Gentian, closed	*Gentiana andrewsii*	**K**
Gerardia, purple	*Agalinis purpurea*	**K**

Gerardia, slender	Agalinis tenuifolia	K
Goatsbeard, yellow	Tragopogon dubius	K
Goldenrod	Solidago spp.	K-I-G
Goldenrod, Gillman's	Solidago simplex	K
Goldenrod, lance-leaved	Euthamia graminifolia	K
Goldenrod, showy	Solidago speciosa	K
Goldenrod, tall	Solidago altissima	K
Harebell	Campanula rotundifolia	K
Hawkweed, orange	Hieracium aurantiacum	A-I
Hawkweed, field	Hieracium caespitosum	K
Hawkweed, mouse-ear	Hieracium pilosella	K
Heal-all, Self-heal	Prunella vulgaris	A-I-K
Heather, false, Beach heath	Hudsonia tomentosa	K
Helleborine	Epipactis helleborine	K-A
Hepatica, round-lobed	Hepatica americana	K
Hog peanut	Amphicarpa bracteata	G
Honeysuckle, glaucous	Lonicera dioica	K
Horehound, water	Lycopus americanus	K
Horsemint	Monarda punctata	K-I
Horsetail	Equisetum sp.	I
Horsetail, field	Equisetum arvense	K
Horsetail rough	Equisetum hiemale	K
Horsetail, smooth	Equisetum levigatum	K
Horseweed	Erigeron canadensis	K
Iris, yellow	Iris pseudacorus	A-I-K
Jack-in-the Pulpit	Arisaema triphyllum	K
Japanese knotweed	Polygonum cuspidatum	A-I
Jewelweed, Spotted touch-me-not	Impatiens capensis	I-K-G
Joe-Pye weed	Eupatorium maculatum.	K-I
Jumpseed, Virginia knotweed	Polygonum virginianum	K
Knapweed, spotted	Centaurea maculosa	A-I-K
Ladies'-tresses, nodding	Spiranthes cernua	K
Ladies'-tresses, slender	Spiranthes gracilis	K
Lady's Slipper, pink, Moccasin flower	Cypripedium acaule	K
Lemon balm	Melissa officianalis	G
Lobelia, brook , Kalm's	Lobelia kalmii	K
Lobelia, great blue	Lobelia siphilitica L.	K
Lobelia, pale-spike	Lobelia spicata	K
Lily, bullhead	Nuphar luteum	I
Lily, water	Nymphaea sp.	I
Lily of the valley, wild, Canada mayflower	Maianthemum canadense	K
Little blue stem	Andropogon scoparius	K
May-apple, Mandrake	Podophyllum peltatum	K
Marsh (or Water) Speedwell	Veronica anagallis-aquatica	A-G

Meadowrue, early	*Thalictrum dioicum*	**K**
Meadowrue, tall	*Thalictrum polyganum*	**G**
Milkweed, common	*Asclepias syriaca*	**K-I**
Milkweed, swamp	*Asclepia incarnata*	**K-G**
Mint, wild	*Mentha arvensis*	**K**
Monkey flower	*Mimulus ringens*	**K**
Motherwort	*Leonurus cardiaca*	**A-I-K**
Morning glory, wild	*Convolvulus sepium*	**I**
Mullein, common	*Verbascum, thapsus*	**A-I-K**
Mullein, moth	*Verbascum blattaria*	**A-I-K**
Mustard, Wormseed, Treacle	*Erysimum cheiranthoides*	**K**
Nettle, hyssop hedge	*Stachys hyssopifolia*	**K**
Niteshade	*Solanum dulcamara*	**A-I-G**
Nightshade, common	*Solanum nigrum*	**K**
Nodding bur marigold	*Bidens cernuus*	**K**
Nightshade, enchanter's	*Circaea quadrisulcata*	**K**
Partridgeberry	*Mitchella repens*	**K**
Pea, everlasting, perennial	*Lathyrus latifolius*	**K**
Pickerel weed	*Pontederia cordata*	**I**
Pipsissewa, Prince's pine	*Chimaphila umbellata*	**K**
Plantain, common	*Plantago major*	**K**
Plantain, English	*Plantago lanceolata*	**K**
Poor man's pepper	*Lepidium virginicum*	**I**
Pokeweed	*Phytolacca americana*	**K-I**
Primrose, evening	*Oenothera biennis*	**K-I**
Puccoon, hairy	*Lithospermum caroliniense*	**K**
Puccoon, hoary	*Lithospermum canescena*	**K**
Purple Loosestrife	*Lythrum salicaria*	**A-K-I-G**
Queen Anne's Lace	*Daucus carota*	**A-I-K**
Ragweed	*Ambrosia artemesilifolia*	**K-G**
Reed grass	*Phragmites communis*	**I**
Reed grass, sand	*Calamovilfa longifolia*	**K**
Rose, smooth	*Rosa blanda*	**K**
Rose Pogonia	*Pogonia ophioglossoides*	**K**
Rushes	*Juncus sp.*	**I**
St. John's Wort, common	*Hypericum perforatum*	**A-I-K**
St. John's Wort, Canada	*Hypericum canadense*	**K**
St. John's Wort, marsh	*Triadenum virginicum (L.) Raf.*	**K**
Sarsaparilla, wild	*Aralia nudicaulis*	**K**
Sedges	*Carex spp.*	**K-I**
Skullcap, mad-dog	*Scutellaria lateriflora*	**K**
Skullcap, marsh	*Scutellaria epilobiifolia*	**K**
Silverweed	*Potentilla anserina*	**K**

Shaggy mane fungi	*Basidium*	I
Snakeroot, white	*Eupatoriaum rugosum*	I
Smartweed	*Polygonum sp.*	I
Solomon's Seal, true	*Polygonatum bifloru*	K
Solomon's Seal, false	*Smilacina racemosa*	K
Solomon's Seal, starry false	*Smilacina stellata*	K
Spring beauty	*Claytonia virginica*	K
Spurge, flowering	*Euphorbia corollata*	K
Strawberry, common	*Fragaria virginiana*	K
Storksbill	*Erodium circutarium*	A-I
Squirrel-corn	*Dicentra canadensis*	K
Sweet cicely	*Ozmorhiza claytonii*	K-I
Toadflax, Dalmatian	*Linaria dalmatica*	K
Teasel	*Dipsacus sylvestris*	I
Thimbleweed	*Anemone virginiana*	K
Thistles	*Cirsium sp.*	I
Thistle, bull	*Cirsium vulgare*	K
Thistle, Pitcher's	*Cirsium pitcheri*	K-T
Thistle, swamp	*Cirsium muticum*	K
Trillium, large flowered	*Trillium grandiflorum*	K
Trout Lily, Adder's tongue, Dogtooth Violet		
	Erythronium americanum	K
Twinflower	*Linnaea borealis*	K
Violet, Canada	*Viola canadensis*	K
Violet, northern white	*Viola pallens*	K
Violet, smooth yellow	*Viola pennsylvanica*	K
Violet, long spurred	*Viola rostrata*	K
Violet, common blue	*Viola papilionacea*	K-A
Violet, cream, pale	*Viola striata*	K
Violet, downy yellow	*Viola pubescens*	K
Viper's bugloss, Blueweed	*Echium vulgare*	A-I
Water parsnip	*Sium suave*	I
Willow-herb, great hairy	*Epilobium hirsutum*	I
Willow-herb, purple-leaved	*Epilobium coloratum*	K
Wintergreen (checkerberry)	*Gaultheria procumbens*	K
Wintergreen, spotted	*Chimaphila maculata*	K
Wood-betony	*Pedicularis canadensis*	K
Wood sage; Germander	*Teucrium canadense L.*	K
Wood sorrel, yellow	*Oxalis fontana Bunge*	K
Wormwood , Mugwort	*Artemisia vulgaris*	A-I
Wormwood	*Artemisia campestris*	K
Wormwood, tall	*Artemisia caudata*	K
Yarrow	*Achillea millefolium*	K-I

Identifying Non-Blooming Plants

Trillium, *Trillium grandiflorum.*   **Jack-in-the-Pulpit**, *Arisaema triphyllum*

Note difference in vein pattern in leaves to tell these K-LDP **woodland plants** apart when not blooming.

These 2 **deep water plants**, found at HI and EGRP, also have very different leaf vein patterns as well as different flowers.

Arrow Arum, *Peltandra virginica.*   **Duck Potato**, *Sagittaria latifolia,* also called **Wapato** or **Broad-Leaved Arrowhead**

Aliens Among Us:
Good, Bad, and Indifferent

Alien species have had a "bad rap" lately. An "alien" or exotic, species is one that is not naturally found growing or living in an area. Many **migrated from Europe or Asia** with people or arrived on ships carrying trade goods. Without the predators that kept them in check in their native lands, some of them became pests. On the master "species lists", both for plants and animals, such species are coded with an **A**.

The "Bad"

Zebra Mussels on beach

Many are harmful and indeed -- infamous. For instance the dreaded **Zebra Mussel** has left shells on the beaches at all 3 *GHWVG* sites. Equally as harmful is the albeit beautiful plant **Purple Loosestrife**, originally brought for gardens, but later "escaping" and invading wetland habitats. It is also found in all 3 of our sites. **Spotted Knapweed** is another pretty plant with purple blossoms that is very harmful, especially at K-LDP where it is a serious menace to other dune species. It is also found at HI.

These descriptions are reprinted with permission from *Alien Invaders*, distributed by the **White Pine Chapter** of **Michigan Botanical Club**.

Purple Loosestrife

"Purple Loosestrife --
Lythrum salicaria

A perennial with handsome tall, purple "spike" flowers, this plant can grow up to 6 feet tall and is an escaped garden plant. Once it gets established in a wetland, it can rapidly outcompete native vegetation, **displacing** and shading out important **wetland** wildlife **plants**. The mature plants have tremendous seed-producing capabilities, averaging 2.7 million seeds per plant. Seeds remain viable for at least 3 years, and can be a big problem for wetlands connected by a common channel, due to seed dispersal by water. Seeds also disperse by clinging to feet of waterfowl and then "riding" to new wetlands, where they germinate and colonize. It was introduced on purpose from Europe, N. Africa, and Asia as a garden flower.

On Oct. 23, 1995, the Michigan legislature enacted a law making it **illegal to sell** most cultivars of Purple Loosestrife. As of Jan. 1, 1997, only completely sterile cultivars can be legally sold. This must be authenticated by the Dept. of Agriculture. Altho advertised as "a sterile hybrid, one that cannot reproduce by seed," it is believed by botanists that these do cross-breed with wild varieties and hence, spread the pest.

"**Alternatives to Purple Loosestrife in the home landscape** may be DragonHead (*Dracocephalem spp.*), a non-invasive ornamental, native *Liatris spp.* (Blazing Star), New York Ironweed, *Vernonia noveboracensis*, a moisture loving plant; or *Physotegia*, Obedient Plant. All have tall spikes of bright pink to purple flowers and can fill a similar "niche" in the home garden.

"Spotted Knapweed --
Centaurea maculosa

A biennial up to four feet tall with round, attractive purplish-pink flowers, this plant feels coarse to touch. Spotted Knapweed **chemically alters** the soil it inhabits, making the soil unsuitable for other plants, resulting in monocultures of spotted knapweed and complete loss of desirable vegetation, such as grasses. With excellent seed manufacturing characteristics, a single plant may produce 400--500 seeds per year that remain viable in the soil for five years or more. Found mostly in disturbed, dry, gravelly, or sandy soil, it was **introduced by accident** from Europe as a contaminant in hay."

"Multiflora Rose --
Rosa multiflora

"Multiflora Rose, found at K-LDP, and Rugosa Rose, found at HI, are both alien species that spread and take over habitat where more beneficial native species could grow.

"Multiflora Rose is a perennial shrub growing in clumps of long arching thorny branches, the tips of which may root when touching the ground. The 1 to 1-½ inch white flowers are usually in pyramidal groups appearing in June and July, followed by bright red fruit which often lasts until spring.

"A native of eastern Asia, it was introduced as an ornamental and used horticulturally as hardy rootstock on which to graft other ornamental varieties. The large thick bushes are sometimes used as 'buffer areas' along superhighways. They also are found on waysides, hedge rows, clearings, and beside woods, where seeds have been distributed by birds and small animals after eating the fruit."

Other "harmful" aliens

Another plant species found in our sites that has been declared by experts to be harmful is **Tartarian Honeysuckle,** found at EGRP and many other wooded areas. This alien is often very prevalent, using soil nutrients and water that could be otherwise used by native species.

Common St. John's Wort, not to be confused with many native

St. John's Wort species, is found at HI and K-LDP. *Hypericum perforatum* has black spots on the yellow petals, along the edges ONLY, which distinguishes it from the native species, which have no spots or spots throughout the petals. This plant is considered by many experts to be among the more serious "invaders." Beekeepers, however, like it as it is a pollen source for honey bees. The other St. John's Worts are all native and not harmful. K-LDP has two other species, **Canada St. John's Wort** which has plain yellow petals with no spots, and **Marsh St. John's Wort**. The marsh species, as its name suggests, is found in wet areas. Its flowers are pink and its leaves are large and clasp the plant's stems.

Helleborine Orchid, found at K-LDP, is another single species that is alien, an invasive garden "escapee," but belongs to a family of otherwise much desired plants -- the orchids. In fact, ALL wild orchids, including the Lady's Slippers and Slender Ladies' Tresses found at K-LDP, are on the **Michigan Protected Species List**. The renegade Helleborine is different only because it was a domestic species originally and not native.

Ragweed is one alien plant that is harmful to many people with allergies. It has been identified at K-LDP. **Nightshade,** found at EGRP and HI, is poisonous. And then there is **dandelion**, found at all 3 sites, which is considered a nuisance by most people, except possibly those who like to make dandelion wine.

Harmful Alien Animals

Zebra mussels are the most infamous of the harmful alien animals that have been seen at our 3 sites.

Mute Swan

Another that can be found at EGRP is the **Mute Swan**. These huge birds were originally a domestic species that "went wild." They are very aggressive and usually drive other waterfowl out of the area where they nest, often preventing other, native species, like Canada Geese, from nesting. They can also be dangerous and will attack humans and pets.

Starlings, originally from Europe, are found at all 3 *GHWVG* sites and are considered by many people to be a nuisance.

The Beetle and The Loosestrife

In 1998 Michigan State University began a program of involving elementary students around the state in a project -- that if successful -- would limit the growth of Purple Loosestrife in Michigan's wetlands. **Bob Swanson's class at Ferry School** in Grand Haven was one chosen to participate.

gallerucella beetle eating purple loosestrife

Since the plant is native to Europe and Asia, it had **no natural predators** when it escaped from gardens and became established in the wild in North America. In Europe a beetle species feeds on the plant and helps control its spread. That beetle, *Galerucella calmariensis*, was tested by MSU entomologists. They needed to be certain that it wouldn't begin eating native plants when its primary food source diminished. Once satisfied that it posed no danger to native vegetation, a pilot program of release was done. Then the project expanded to include Michigan school children; 30 classrooms state-wide were selected for participation

Swanson's mixed level class of 3rd, 4th, and 5th graders **raised** purple loosestrife with the **beetles in their classroom** and the school's courtyard. In its larva and adult stages the beetle munches on the leaves and stems of loosestrife.

First released in EGRP, a later batch was let go at HI.

Swanson's 1997 **class** "adopted" **EGRP** as a project, where they performed "clean up" duties, removing litter and at the same time observing the wildlife and ecological interactions that occurred there. That 1997 class supplied the author with a list of animals they had observed, which is included in the various species lists of *GHWVG*.

The two projects demonstrate how preserved natural areas can serve an educational purpose, both in "watching wildlife" and "scientific research."

Of the beetle project, **Swanson comments**, "In my 20 some years of teaching I have found nothing that came as close to motivating my students as the Purple Loosestrife Project. They saw first-hand their relationship and their responsibility to the natural world. They felt a sense of empowerment and pride in what they were doing. They wanted to learn as much as they could and to share their knowledge and concern with others. I'm sure it's an experience that will impact the rest of their lives."

The "Good"
Ring-Necked Pheasant

Butter and Eggs, found at K-LDP, is a host species for the **Buckeye Butterfly**, along with the native *Linaria* species. The **Ring-Necked Pheasant**, found sometimes at K-LDP, is a game bird that was introduced for that purpose. In recent years its numbers have declined due largely to changes in farming practices. Early mowing of fields, before nesting season is complete, have wiped out many pheasant nests. With less space being left to tall grasses between fields in farmed areas, their habitat has further been reduced.

Butter and Eggs:

The "Indifferent"

Black Locust (*Robinia pseudoacacia*) is a fast growing, medium sized (30 to 40 foot) tree with a vigorous wide-spreading root system, found on HI. It is considered by some to be **among the most harmful** of the alien species. Bunches of showy fragrant white flowers appear in May and June. The fruit is a legume which forms in late autumn and remains on the branches throughout the winter.

It originated in the Appalachian Mountains and the Ozark Region. Because this tree is the most **common caterpillar food plant for the silver spotted skipper,** our largest skipper butterfly, its position on the harmful list is debatable to some ecologists.

Arguments can be started over whether some species are harmful. **Baby's Breath,** for instance, has seriously endangered populations of the **Threatened Pitcher's Thistle** farther north in Michigan. A popular plant with flower arrangers, it is often grown in yards and then escapes. Because it has a "tumbleweed like" method of distributing its seeds, it can blow great distances. K-LDP is one of two sites (the other is not a *MWVG* site) in the Grand Haven area that have flourishing populations of the threatened Pitcher's Thistle. It would be tragic if these populations were to become endangered by rampaging Baby's Breath. Fortunately it hasn't yet been identified growing in any of our sites.

One of the author's personal favorites is **Common Mullein,** *Verbascum thapsus,* which has been claimed by some experts to be a harmful alien. This beautiful plant can grow up to 8 feet tall. The flowers bloom differentially, with only part of them in blossom at a time, promoting a longer pollination season. The seeds on the tall stalks are much prized by birds, especially finches, which also eat thistle seed.

Originally brought from Europe as a garden plant, mullein has a lengthy, interesting **folklore history.** Ancient Romans dipped the dried stalks in tallow and used them for torches. Since it arrived with early settlers on this continent, it spread and became an important plant for Native Americans. They lined moccasins with the soft leaves to keep their feet warm. They also heated the leaves on fired rocks and then wrapped sprained ankles and other joints with them. Probably the most significant use was to boil the leaves and make a steam which, when inhaled, **relieved lung congestion.** Medical research has determined that the plant's leaves do contain mucilage which provides verified relief of lung congestion.

Bouncing Bet, also called Soapwort, because its roots make "suds" in water, is another alien species long included in natural folklore. It is found at all 3 of our sites.

Both these plants can be picked with impunity and used for teaching purposes for school classes, scout troops, or other youth groups.

Other such "aliens" found at our sites include **hoary alyssum, hawkweed, heal-all** or self heal, **Queen Anne's lace** and **Viper's bugloss.**

Finding and identifying an "alien" plant can be just as challenging to novice botanists as the more rare or "special" plants.

If a person is making a **personal herbarium** -- a scrapbook of pressed plant specimens -- for a school study, or making craft items from pressed plants, these plants may be picked and used without harming the environment.

Population Shifts

Before we get into endangered and threatened species, it might be appropriate to discuss how animal and plant population numbers and distributions have changed.

Northern Cardinal

Well known Muskegon naturalist and newspaper columnist, **Margaret Drake Elliott**, once commented that when she arrived in the Muskegon area in the late 1920s, it was rare to see a cardinal. By the 1980s when the author met her, they were common and still are. In her book, *A Number of Things*, she explains how this came about. At the beginning of the century, she states, they were a southern bird, that gradually extended its range until now it covers most of the country East of the Mississippi. It was still not frequently found north of a line from Muskegon to Saginaw.

While an extension of range of a beautiful bird such as the cardinal, found in all 3 *GHWVG* sites, is good news, a decline in range is far more frequent for many bird species.

As human populations continue to expand exponentially, territory for suitable wildlife habitat decreases.

Eastern Bluebirds, Wood Ducks and **Tree Swallows**, all to be found in *GHWVG* sites, are examples of birds that normally nest in cavities in dead trees. As natural wooded areas diminished, their nesting sites did also. It was up to humans to replace the natural nest sites with nest boxes of appropriate size and height. Since this has occurred, all 3 species have begun to recover.

Tom Hendrickson, former president of **MAS**, told Holland Audubon Club (HAC) in the late 1990s, "At one time there were 12 million **Red-winged Blackbirds** in Michigan; today there are 6 million." Since they (also found in *GHWVG* sites) are primarily a species of wetland edges, as wetlands decrease they too are losing favored habitat.

Once there were millions of **Passenger Pigeons** in Grand Haven. In fact, Spring Lake artist Lewis Cross painted them en mass. Today they are extinct.

In recent years, several attempts have been made to introduce legislation that would legalize the hunting of mourning doves in Michigan. An argument in favor of this quotes the 37 states that already have such hunting. Again Tom Hendrickson explains why this isn't practical for Michigan. (see pg. 57)

Already **endangered** are Peregrine Falcon and King Rail, both mentioned elsewhere in *GHWVG*. Peregrine Falcons are recovering, especially due to being raised and released. Two that nested in 2001 at HI were reared in Wisconsin.

Habitats such as *GHWVG* sites may prove to be the last refuge for species in the future.

Being Lost?

There appears to be only one **plant species** found in our sites that is **threatened**, the Pitcher's Thistle.

Pitcher's
Thistle

This information comes from the DNR list filed on March 5, 1999. It is **illegal to remove** any plant or animal on this list from its natural habitat, per section 36503 of Act No. 451 of the Public Acts of 1994, as amended, of Michigan Compiled Laws. This list is updated periodically when species are added or deleted.

However our sites have several declining birds. **Threatened** are: Least Bittern, Caspian Tern, Common Tern, Osprey, and Bald Eagle.

References

Books listed include those used for research for this book, as well as general reference books. A good field guide for identification is recommended. Some use drawings; others, photographs. Many contain range maps, showing where the species is most likely to be found. It is a personal choice which one a "wildlife viewer" prefers to use in positively identifying a plant or animal. Some of the books listed include information on behavior or habitat, which may provide further insight into the location of the plant or animal. The books listed include a cross section of primarily currently available references. There are many other excellent sources. The information printed with each listing should be adequate for ordering from a book store or library. Some of the best references are available only from the organization that published them, however. Most of the listed references are on Michigan, Mid-West, or Eastern North American species. Some cover a broader geographic area, such as the whole continent of North America. Those that mention a different state or Canada include species found in West Michigan and are listed because they are excellent sources of information on these species. Some books are on auxiliary information, such as habitat types or animal tracks or evidence.

Birds

American Ornithologists' Union. **Check-List of North American Birds: The Species of Birds of North America from the Arctic through Panama, including the West Indies and Hawaiian Islands. Seventh Edition.** American Ornithologists' Union. Washington D.C. 1998. no illustrations. **Note:** This is the reference by which the bird list in *GHWVG* is organized.

Bent, Arthur Cleveland. **Life Histories of North American Gulls and Terns.** Dover Publications Inc. New York. 1963.

Brewer, Richard, McPeak, Gail A., and Adams, Raymond J. Jr. **Atlas of Breeding Birds of Michigan.** MSU Press. East Lansing. 1991. range maps. drawings.

Bull, John and Ferrand, John Jr. **The Audubon Society Field Guide to North American Birds: Eastern Region.** Alfred A. Knopf. New York. 1992. color photos. range maps.

Clark, William S. & Wheeler, Brian K. **A Field Guide to Hawks of North America.** Houghton Mifflin Co. Boston. 1987. B & W and color

Black-capped Chickadee

Dark-eyed (slate-colored) Junco

drawings, B & W photos, range maps.

Dunn, Jon, and Garrett, Kimball. **A Field Guide to Warblers of North America**. Houghton Mifflin Co. Boston. 1997. color photos and drawings. range maps.

Dunne, Pete. **The Wind Masters: The Lives of North American Birds of Prey.** Houghton Mifflin Co. Boston. 1995. B & W drawings.

Ehrlich, Paul R., Dobkin, David S., & Wheye, Darryl. **The Birders' Handbook: A Field Guide to the Natural History of North American Birds -- The Essential Companion to Your Identification Guide.** Simon & Schuster, Inc. New York. 1988. drawings. icons.

Gillette, John, & Mohrhardt, David. **Coat Pocket Bird Book: A Field Guide to Birding.** Thunder Bay Press. Lansing. 1995. color drawings.

Gooders, John & Weindensaul, Scott. **The Practical Ornithologist: What to look for, how and when to look for it, and how to record what you see.** Simon & Schuster, Inc. New York. 1990. color & B & W photos and drawings.

Harrison, Hal H. **A Field Guide to the Birds' Nests: United States east of the Mississippi River.** Houghton Mifflin Co. Boston. 1975. color photos & B & W drawings.

Harrison, Kit & George. **America's Favorite Backyard Birds.** Simon & Schuster. New York. 1983. B & W photos.

Hochbaum, H. Albert. **Travels and Traditions of Waterfowl.** Charles T. Branford Co. Newton, MA. 1955. drawings.

Kaufman, Kenn. **A Field Guide to Advanced Birding: Birding Challenges and How to Approach Them.** Houghton Mifflin Co. Boston. 1990. drawings.

Kortright, Francis H. **The Ducks, Geese and Swans of**

Blue Jay

North America. Stackpole Co. Harrison, PA. 1967. drawings. range and migration maps.

House Finch

National Geographic Society. **Field Guide to the Birds of North America. Second Edition.** National Geographic Society. Washington, D.C. 1994. color drawings. range maps.

Pasquier, Roger F. **Watching Birds: An Introduction to Ornithology.** Houghton Mifflin Co. Boston. 1977. drawings.

Peterson, Roger Tory. **Peterson First Guide to Birds of North America.** Houghton Mifflin Co. Boston. 1986. color drawings.

Peterson, Roger Tory. **A Field Guide to the Birds: A Completely New Guide to All the Birds of Eastern and Central North America. Fourth Edition.** Houghton Mifflin Co., Boston. 1980. color drawings. range maps.

Ponshair, James. **Birds of Ottawa County.** Lill & Jim Budzynski, publisher. Coopersville, MI. 1998. B & W drawings and photos.

Rising, James D. **A Guide to the Identification and Natural History of The Sparrows of the United States and Canada.** Academic Press. 1996. drawings. range maps.

Robbins, Chandler S., Bruun, Bertel, & Zim, Herbert S. **A Guide to Field Identification Birds of North America, expanded, revised edition.** Golden Press. New York. 1983. color drawings. range maps.

Short, Lester L. **The Lives of Birds: Birds of the World and Their Behavior.** Henry Holt & Co. New York. 1993. color photos & B & W drawings.

Stokes, Donald W. **A Guide to Bird Behavior, Vol. I.** Little, Brown & Co., Boston. 1979. B & W drawings. migration maps.

Stokes, Donald W. and Lillian Q. **A Guide to Bird Behavior: in the wild and at your feeder. Vol. II.** Little Brown & Co. Boston. 1983. B & W drawings. migration maps.

Stokes, Donald W. & Lillian Q. **A Guide to Bird Behavior, Vol. III.** Little, Brown & Co. Boston. 1989. B & W drawings. migration maps.

Tekielo, Stan. **Birds of Michigan: Field Guide**. Adventure Publications. Cambridge, MN. 1999. color photos. range maps.

Zim, Herbert S. & Gabrielson, Ira N. Birds: **A Guide to Familiar American Birds**. Golden Press. New York. 1987. color drawings, range maps.

Zimmerman, Dale A., & Van Tyne, Josselyn. **A Distributional Check-list of The Birds of Michigan.** University of Michigan Museum of Zoology. Ann Arbor. 1959. no illustrations.

Goldfinch

Animals Other Than Birds

Babcock, Harold L. **Turtles of the Northeastern United States.** Dover Publications, Inc. New York. 1971. color drawings.

Behler, John L. **The Audubon Society Field Guide to North American Reptiles & Amphibians.** Alfred A. Knopf. New York. 1979. color photos. range maps.

Bradt, G.W., Schafer, Charles E., & Harrington, Steve. **Wildlife Sketches**. Martitime Press. St. Ignance. 1999. (Previously published as **Michigan Wildlife Sketches: the Native Mammals of Michigan's Forests, Fields, and Marshes.** Michigan Dept. of Natural Resources. Lansing. 1972.) drawings.

Burt, William Henry. **A Field Guide to the Mammals of North America north of Mexico.** Houghton Mifflin. Boston. 1980. drawings. photos. range maps.

Burt, Wm. H. **Mammals of the Great Lakes Region.** 1972. University of Michigan Press. Ann Arbor. drawings. range maps.

Carr, Archie. **Handbook of Turtles: The Turtles of the United States, Canada, and Baja California.** Cornell University Press. Ithaca. 1952. range maps. B & W photos.

Carter, David. **Eyewitness Handbooks Butterflies and Moths.** Dorling Kindersley, Inc. New York. 1992. color drawings & photos. range maps.

Daccordi, Maura, Triberti, Paolo, & Zanetti, Adriano. **Guide to Butterflies & Moths.** Simon & Schuster, Inc. New York. 1987. color photos. icons.

Dunn, Gary A. **Insects of the Great Lakes Region.** 1996. University of Michigan Press. drawings. identification keys.

Elman, Robert. **The Hunter's Field Guide to the Game Birds and Animals of North America.** 1974. Alfred A. Knopf. New York. color & B & W photos.

Evers, David C. **A Guide to Michigan's Endangered Wildlife.** 1992. University of Michigan Press. Ann Arbor. color photos. range maps.

Halfpenny, James. **A Field Guide to Mammal Tracking in North America.** 1986. Johnson Books. Boulder. drawings.

Harding, James H & Holman, J. Alan. **Michigan Frogs, Toads, and Salamanders.** 1992. Cooperative Extension Service, Michigan State University. East Lansing. color photos. range maps.

Harding, James H., and Holman, J. Alan. **Michigan Turtles and Lizards.** 1990. Michigan State University. East Lansing. color photos. range maps.

Headstrom, Richard.

Suburban Wildlife: An Introduction to the Common Animals of Your Back Yard and Local Park. 1984. Prentice Hall. Englewood Cliffs, N.J. drawings.

Holman, J. Alan, Harding, James H., Hensley, Marvin M., and Dudderar, Glenn R.

Eastern Box Turtle, species of special concern

Michigan Snakes: A Field Guide and Pocket Reference. Cooperative Extension Service. Michigan State University. East Lansing. color photos. drawings. range maps.

Kurta, Allen. **Mammals of the Great Lakes Region.** 1995. University of Michigan Press. Ann Arbor. B & W photos. drawings. range maps.

Murie, Olaus J. **A Field Guide to Animal Tracks.** 1975. Houghton Mifflin Co. Boston. drawings.

Nielsen, Mogens C. **Michigan Butterflies & Skippers: A Field Guide and Reference.** MSU. East Lansing. 1999. color photos. range maps.

Nowicki, Tim. **Awake to Wildlife: The Complete Naturalist's Great Lakes Wildlife Almanac.** 1994. Glovebox Guidebooks Publishing Co. Clarkston, MI. drawings.

Pyle, Robert Michael. **The Audubon Society Field Guide to North American Butterflies.** Alfred A. Knopf. New York. 1981. color photos.

Pyle, Robert Michael. **Handbook for Butterfly Watchers.** Houghton Mifflin Co. Boston. 1984. drawings.

Scott, W. B. & Crossman, E.J. **Freshwater Fishes of Canada.** Fisheries Research Board of Canada. Ottawa. 1973. drawings. range maps. key.

Stall, Chris. **Animals Tracks of the Great Lakes States.** 1989. The Mountaineers. Seattle. drawings.

Stokes, Donald & Lillian. **Field Guide to Animal Tracking & Behavior.** Little Brown & Co. Boston.

Whitaker, John O. Jr. **The Audubon Society Field Guide to North American Mammals.** Alfred A. Knopf. New York. 1980. color photos. range maps.

Wright, Amy Bartlett. **Peterson First Guide to Caterpillars of North America.** Houghton Mifflin Co. Boston. 1993. color drawings.

Plant References

Angier, B. **Field Guide to Edible Wild Plants.** Stackpole Books. Harrisburg, PA. 1974. drawings.

Sand Cherries found at K-LDP make good jam

Angier, B. **Field Guide To Medicinal Wild Plants.** Stackpole Books. Harrisburg, PA. 1978. drawings.

Arora, David. **Mushrooms Demystified.: A Comprehensive Guide to the Fleshy Fungi.** Ten Speed Press. Berkeley. 1986. color & B & W photos.

Bland, John H. **Forests of Lilliput: The Realm of Mosses & Lichens.** Prentice-Hall, Inc. Englewood Cliffs, NJ. 1971. B & W photos. drawings.

Billington, Cecil. **Shrubs of Michigan.** Cranbrook Institute. Bloomfield Hills. 1977. drawings. range maps.

Britton, Lord N & Brown, A. **An Illustrated Flora of the Northern United States and Canada Volume I (Ferns to Buckwheat).** Dover Publications, Inc. New York. 1913. drawings.

Britton, Lord N & Brown, A. **An Illustrated Flora of the Northern United States and Canada Volume II (Amaranth to Polypremum)** Dover Publications, Inc. New York. 1913. drawings.

Britton, Lord N & Brown, A. **An Illustrated Flora of the Northern United States and Canada Volume III (Gentian to Thistle)** Dover Publications, Inc. New York. 1913. drawings.

Poison Ivy

Brown, L. **Grasses: An Identification Guide.** Houghton Mifflin Co. Boston. 1979. drawings.

Cobb, B. **Ferns.** Houghton Mifflin. Boston. 1963. drawings.

Courtenay, B. & Zimmerman, J. H. **Wildflowers and Weeds.** Prentice Hall Press. New York. 1978. photos.

Crum, Howard. **Liverworts and Hornworts of Southern Michigan.** U of M. Ann Arbor, MI. 1991. no illustrations.

Dana, Mrs. W. S. **How to Know the Wild Flowers.** Houghton Mifflin Co. Boston. 1893. drawings

Darlington, Henry T. **The Mosses of Michigan.** Cranbrook Institute of Science. Bloomfield Hills, MI. 1964. drawings. identification keys.

Eastman, John. **The Book of Swamp and Bog: Trees, Shrubs, and Wildflowers of Eastern Freshwater Wetlands.** Stackpole Books. Mechanicsburg, PA. 1995. drawings.

Edsall, M. S. **Roadside Plants and Flowers.** U. of Wisconsin Press. Madison. 1985. photos.

American Bittersweet

Elias, T. S & Dykeman, P. A. **Field Guide to North American Edible Wild Plants.** Outdoor Life Books. New York. 1982. photos.

Emberton, J. **PODS: Wildflowers and Weeds in Their Final Beauty.** Charles Scribner's Sons. New York. 1979. photos.

Fassett, N. C. **Spring Flora of Wisconsin.** University of Wisconsin Press. Madison, WI 1976. drawings. identification keys.

Ferguson, M. & Saunders, R. M. **Wildflowers Through the Seasons.** Arrowood Press. New York. 1989. photos

Fernald, M. L. **Gray's Manual of Botany.** Dioscorides Press. Portland OR. 1950. drawings.

Forey, P. **American Nature Guides Wild Flowers.** Gallery Books. New York. 1990. drawings.

Foster, S & Duke, J. A. **Eastern / Central Medicinal Plants.** Houghton Mifflin Co. Boston. 1990. drawings & photos.

Gleason, H.A. & Cronquist, A. **Manual of Vascular Plants of Northeastern United States and Adjacent Canada, Second Edition.** The New York Botanical Garden. New York. 1991. no illustrations or range maps.

Glime, Janice M. **The Elfin World of Mosses and Liverworts of Michigan's Upper Peninsula and Isle Royale Isle** Royale Natural History Assoc. 1993. color photos.

Hoagman, Walter J. **A Field Guide Great Lakes Coastal Plants.** MSU Cooperative Extension Service. 1994. drawings.

Knobel, E. **Field Guide to the Grasses, Sedges and Rushes of the United States.** Dover Publications. New York. 1980. drawings.

Levine, Carol. **A Guide to Wildflowers in Winter: Herbaceous Plants of Northeastern North America.** Yale University Press. New Haven. 1995. drawings.

Lund, H. C. **Michigan Wildflowers In Color.** Village Press. Traverse City, MI. 1988, 1991. photos.

Sassafras

Medlin, Julie Jones. **Michigan Lichens.** Cranbrook Institute of Science. Bloomfield Hills, MI. 1996. color photos.

Miller, Orson K. Jr. **Mushrooms of North America.** E. P. Dutton & Co., Inc. New York. 1970. color photos.

Newcomb, L. **Newcomb's Wildflower Guide.** Little, Brown and Co. Boston. 1977. drawings.

Niering, W.A. **The Audubon Society Field Guide to North American Wildflowers.** Alfred A. Knopf, New York. 1979. photos.

Otis, C. H. **Michigan Trees.** University of Michigan Press. Ann Arbor. 1978. photos.

Peterson, R. T., McKenny, M., **A Field Guide to Wildflowers of Northeastern and North-central North America.** Houghton Mifflin Co., Boston. 1968. drawings.

Petrides, G. A. **A Field Guide to Trees and Shrubs.** Houghton Mifflin Co. Boston. 1972. drawings.

Rabeler, Richard K. **Gleason's Plants of Michigan.** Oakleaf Press. Ann Arbor, MI. 1998. drawings.

Reader's Digest. **North American Wildlife Trees and Nonflowering plants.** Reader's Digest Assoc. Pleasantville. 1998. color drawings. range maps.

Schinkel, Dick & Mohrhardt, David. **Favorite Wildflowers of the Great Lakes and the Northeastern U.S.** Thunder Bay Press, Lansing. 1994. color drawings.

Simonds, Roberta L. & Tweedie, Henrietta H. **Wildflowers of the Great Lakes Region.** Stipes Publishing. 1997. (Previously published as **Wildflowers of Michigan.** 1976.) drawings.

Smith, N. F. **Michigan Trees Worth Knowing.** Hillsdale Educational Publishers, Inc. Hillsdale, MI 1978. drawings

Tekielo, Stan. **Wildflowers of Michigan: Field Guide.** Adventure Publications. Cambridge, MN. 2000. color photos. range maps.

Venning, F. D. **Wildflowers of North America.** Golden Press, New York. 1984. drawings.

Voss, E. G. **Michigan Flora Part I Gymnosperms and Monocots.** Cranbrook Institute of Science. Bloomfield Hills, MI. 1972. drawings, photos, range maps.

Voss, E. G. **Michigan Flora Part II Dicots (Saururaceae -- Cornaceae)** Cranbrook Institute of Science. Bloomfield Hills, MI. 1985. drawings. photos. range maps.

Voss, E. G. **Michigan Flora Part III Dicots (Pyrolaceae -- Compositae)** Cranbrook Institute of Science. Bloomfield Hills, MI. drawings. photos. range maps.

Weatherbee, E. E. & Bruce, J. G. **Edible Wild Plants of The Great Lakes Region.** U. of Michigan. 1979. photos.

White Pine Chapter, Michigan Botanical Club. **Alien Invaders: Invasive Plants.** 2001. Order from WPC, 7951 Walnut, Newaygo, MI 49337-9205. Enclose $2.50 for publication and shipping costs.

· Horsetails

General References

Benyus, Janine M. **Northwoods Wildlife: A Watcher's Guide to Habitats.** 1989. NorthWord Press, Inc. Minocqua, WI.

Benyus, Janine M. **The Field Guide to Wildlife Habitats of the Eastern United States.** 1989. Simon & Schuster, Inc. New York. drawings. range maps. locator charts.

Blocksma, Mary. **Naming Nature: A Seasonal Guide for the Amateur Naturalist.** Penguin Books. New York. 1992. drawings.

Caduto, Michael J. **Pond And Brook: A Guide to Nature in Freshwater Environments.** University Press of New England. Hanover. 1990. B & W photos and drawings.

Cvancara, Alan M. **At the Water's Edge: Nature Study in Lakes, Streams, and Ponds.** John Wiley & Sons, Inc. New York. 1989. B & W photos & drawings.

Dudderar, Glenn. **Nature from Your Back Door.** 1991. Cooperative Extension Service. Michigan State University. East Lansing. drawings.

Elliott, Margaret Drake. **A Number of Things.** Dana Printing Corp. Muskegon, MI. 1984. drawings.

Martin, Alexander , Zim, Herbert S., & Nelson, Arnold L. **American Wildlife & Plants: A Guide to Wildlife Food Habits.** Dover Publications, Inc. New York. 1951. drawings. range maps. charts.

Niering, William A. **Wetlands: a comprehensive field guide of North America's rivers, lakes, and swamps.** Alfred A. Knopf. New York. color photos. drawings. range maps.

Pitcher, Emma Bickham. **Of Woods and Other Things.** Beech Leaf Press. Kalamazoo, MI. 1996. drawings.

Pitcher, Emma Bickham. **Ramblings: Reflections on Nature.** Beech Leaf Press. Kalamazoo, MI. 2001. drawings.

Tillman, Elizabeth Brockwell, & Wolf, Earl. **Discovering Great Lakes Dunes.** MSU Cooperative Extension Service. 1998. color photos.

Abbreviations Used

Icons for sites:
K = Kitchel-Lindquist Dunes Preserve; **I** = Harbor Island; **G** = East Grand River Park

Site Abbreviations:
K-LDP = Kitchel-Lindquist Dunes Preserve; **HI** = Harbor Island; **EGRP** = East Grand River Park

Other organizations, grants, or definitions:
AOU, American Ornithologists' Union; **B & W**, black and white as in photos and/or drawings; **CETA,** Comprehensive Employment & Training Act; **CMU,** Central Michigan University; **CZM,** Coastal Zone Management Grants; **DNR,** Michigan Dept. of Natural Resources; **GHACF,** Grand Haven Area Community Foundation; **GVSC & GVSU,** Grand Valley State Colleges & Grand Valley State University; **HAC,** Holland Audubon Club; **MBC,** Michigan Botanical Club; **MSU,** Michigan State University; **MAS,** Michigan Audubon Society; **MYC,** Michigan Youth Corps Grants; **NBCF,** North Bank Community Fund; **NOWS,** North Ottawa Water System; **OIAS,** Owashtanong Islands Audubon Society; **WPC,** White Pine Chapter; **YES,** Youth Employment Services Grant.

Author's Acknowledgments

It is with great trepidation that I set out to write this. No matter how hard I try to remember everyone who has helped make this book possible, someone is sure to be left out. So, up front I apologize to anyone who is overlooked.

The first person I need to recognize is **Marjorie Hendricks**, Grand Haven's foremost environmental expert. Marj first introduced me to the Kitchel Dune. If it hadn't been for her, there probably would be an upscale housing development on that property instead of a publicly owned dune preserve enjoyed by many and useful as an educational site from elementary thru college levels.

Marj spent countless hours observing and recording natural occurrences at the site. Her species lists have been used by several publications, including *GHWVG*.

She was the inspiration and guiding light of a group that ran a **successful petition drive**, forcing a referendum vote where Grand Haven voters chose, by a 3 to 1 margin, to overturn a zoning change that would have allowed development. When the developers were unable to go ahead with their plans, the Nature Conservancy purchased the site.

Marj was always generous -- with me and others -- sharing her considerable knowledge of dune ecology and the plants and animals that inhabited the area. For this opportunity to learn from a real expert, I am eternally grateful.

Another early influence on my environmental education was **Fred Bevis**. When he agreed to be my academic adviser when I enrolled at Grand Valley State Colleges (GVSC) as an environmental sciences major, little did he realize that over 25 years later he would still be advising me! Ever generous with his abundant knowledge of "everything ecological," his information on the plants, birds, and ecological relationships along the Grand River, especially regarding EGRP, have been of inestimable benefit in writing this book. Also he contributed the "heron research" data.

For information on birds, I owe **James Ponshair** of Allendale, considered by most environmentalists to be the "premier birder" of west Michigan. He is the one who made the bird species list that was given to Phil Seng, my first species list, and the Harbor Island Master Plan list. I've lost count of how many times Jim has reviewed my *GHWVG* bird species list.

In fact, it is to Jim that I owe the "Migration Dates" info provided by **George Wickstrom** and used with his permission.

To **Carolyn Kitchel Titus** of Las Vegas, Nevada I owe the organization of the bird species list. She tipped me off on using *A.O.U. Check-list of North American Birds*; "reorganized" my original list to conform to AOU; provided several additional species for the K-LDP site.

Ed Post of Grand Haven, **Steve Menard** of GRAC, and **Roger Tharp**, who also wrote of his birdwatching adventures at HI, went over the list and offered suggestions. **Chip Francke** and **OIAS** allowed reprinting of his peregrine feeding observations.

Yvonne "Vonnie" Way of Spring Lake was ever patient in reviewing and revising the story of the **North American Lotus**, seen from EGRP.

Information on K-LDP was willingly provided by botanist **Sylvia Birckhead** -- who also provided plant species data and identification; MDNR Naturalist **Elizabeth Brockwell-Tillman,** co-author of *Discovering Great Lakes Dunes*; naturalist **Linda Koning** of Zeeland, who shared her lengthy up-to-date plant and butterfly species lists; and **Lynne Kinkema**, current chair of the K-LDP Committee.

Dennis Craun, Ferrysburg City Manager, and **Mitch Diesch**, Grand Haven Assistant City Manager, both checked their municipalities' data for accuracy.

Dr. Mary Jane Dockeray, former director of Blandford Nature Center; **Bob Swanson**, teacher at Ferry Elementary School in Grand Haven; **Bruce Baker; Ruth Drent; John Klaver; Aneta Houts; Harrison Wallace; Larry Kieft; Richard, Lois, Clarence Otto,** and **Wallace Klempel; Mayor Ed Lystra;** Michigan State Senator **Leon Stille;** all provided or were interviewed for their personal experiences or info on background of the sites.

Luckily for me, people who really are knowledgeable are often willing to share their expertise.

Ray Rustem of MDNR Natural Heritage program, which oversees the *MWVG*, provided quotes and information.

Thanks are also due to the voters of the State of Michigan for passing the bill that provided funds to establish the Michigan Natural Resources Trust Fund Grants, which enabled the City of Ferrysburg to purchase K-LDP. And the multiple grants from various taxpayer funded sources that have, over the years, allowed improvements to make the sites all more accessible and available to the general public. And to that "public" who many times turned out for "clean-up" days at the various sites.

Without the technical assistance of **Robert Riepma**, who also wrote the chapter on Gulls, this manuscript never would have been completed.

It is embarrassing to admit how many errors **Charlie Misner** found when he proofed the manuscript. The errors that remain are my responsibility, not his!

And, most of all, my "co-author" **Kelly Jewell**, without whose drawings this book wouldn't be. Not only is she a great artist, but her extensive background in the printing industry was of great benefit. Little did she realize when she agreed to participate in this project, all the additional hassles that are involved in producing a book!

Betty J. Mattson, July, 2001

Information on Author & Illustrator

Betty J. Mattson and **Kelly Jewell** hold the portrait of *Samantha Spring Cackler* and *Summer Lady II* that Jewell painted.

Betty J. Mattson has been writing since she was in grade school, when a poem made it to the county fair. Her articles on animals, nature, and aviation have been published in newspapers and magazines since 1973. She has a B.S. degree in environmental sciences, natural history tract (1976) and a M.Ed. in adult education (1990) from Grand Valley State University. Two more nature books are partially written.

She lives in Grand Haven, MI with her 2 certified therapy dogs, Snoflake and Serendipity. Robert Riepma is her "life partner."

Besides a love of animals and an interest in nature, the two both have high school class reunions during July, 2001 -- the 20th for Jewell, the 40th for Mattson.

Kelly Jewell has been drawing since she was in grade school. She is a veteran of several years working in the printing industry. Currently she lives on a 10 acre farm in Fruitport, Michigan with her husband, 2 daughters, 3 dogs, 3 horses, 4 cats, and multiple chickens. Altho she claims her first love is horses, she specializes in drawing animals, often from photos as she did with the author's dogs shown above.

Index

Species with both common and scientific names, as well as sites where they have been identified, are listed: **Birds**, pgs. 34-38; **Plants**, pgs. 68-74; **Butterflies**, pgs. 18-19. They are cross-referenced in this Index. **References** are listed by author and title on pgs. 84-94. Items included on those lists are not mentioned in this index. Bird, plant, animal species are only listed here if they are referred to in the text and authors and book titles are also listed only where referred to -- or quoted from -- in the text. **Scientific names are not indexed** unless they are used in place of common names. Items are listed by current most frequently used common names and cross referenced with other common names. **Names of organizations** are indexed by initials; the explanation of what these represent is found in the **Abbreviations List** on page 93.

see pages 17-18 for explanation of dune formation

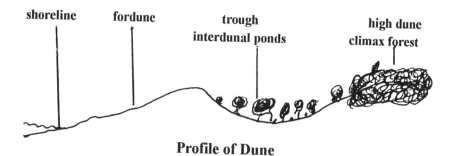

Profile of Dune

Why Not Send Copies of *Grand Haven Wildlife Viewing Guide* to your friends?

Fill out the order blanks on the other side for each person to whom you wish to send *GHWVG*. Enclose a check or money order for $13.00 for each book ordered. This price includes the book; Michigan State Sales Tax, which we are required to collect; first class postage to any U.S. destination; and a "gift card" from you. Each book is mailed in a separate envelope, so we can easily mail to separate addresses from one order. Put additional names on a sheet of paper.

To inquire about "quantity discounts" for orders of 10 books or more shipped to one address, including orders for schools or organizations, contact *Sky Enterprises* **Publications**, 805 Waverly Ave., Grand Haven, MI 49417-2131. Telephone 616-846-4254 or FAX 616-847-0751.

Mail orders to:
Sky Enterprises **Publications**
805 Waverly Ave.
Grand Haven, MI 49417-2131.

Make check or money order payable to *Sky Enterprises*. Usually orders will be shipped same day received; however, if you want the book to arrive later, please indicate this.

Ideas for "gift cards":

To: the Smiths, when you next visit us, we will take you exploring here.

To: Jimmy from Susie. I'll show you some neat animals at one of these sites next time you come to Grand Haven.

Happy Tracking! I know how much you like to hike nature trails and thought this book might give you some new ideas of where to go and what you might see!

For: Leaders of Girl Scout Troop #123 or Youth Explorers, etc.: These sites offer a host of opportunities for neat nature projects and explorations!

GHWVG Order Form

To: _____

Address: _____

City, State, Zip _____

Gift card to read: _____

_____

****

To: _____

Address: _____

City, State, Zip _____

Gift card to read: _____

_____

****

To: _____

Address: _____

City, State, Zip _____

Gift card to read: _____

_____

****

To: _____

Address: _____

City, State, Zip _____

Gift card to read: _____

_____